TABLE OF CONTENTS

Chapter 1. Numbers and Computers 5

    Counting 5

    Computing 7

    Logic 12

    Punch Cards 15

    Television 18

    Early Computers 20

    Mainframes 24

    Programming 27

    Chips 32

    Moore's Law 34

    Personal Computers 36

Chapter 2. Artificial Intelligence 38

    The Turing Test 38

    Research 39

    Applying Artificial Intelligence 42

    Robotics 44

    Drones 54

    3D Printing 58

    Speech Recognition 61

    Singularity 65

    Autonomous Devices 74

    The Brain on a Chip 76

    Humanizing Devices 78

Regulation 79
Chapter 3. Cryptocurrencies 80
Proof of Work 80
Mining for Coins 84
Volatility 85
Proliferation 90
Scrypt 92
Regulators 94
The Future 95
Chapter 4. Blockchain Technology 99
Trust, Consensus, Immutable 99
Chapter 5. Disrupting Commerce 114
Identity Management 116
Music and Publishing 117
Retailers 119
Real Estate 121
Smart Contracts 122
Government 123
Healthcare 125
Insurance and Risk 127
Charities 129
Financial Services 131
Network Support 133
Crowdfunding 134
Ridesharing 136
Logistics - the Ultimate Use of Blockchain Technology 137

Prologue

The need to record transactions among humans became necessary as inhabitants of early civilized villages transferred assets or services.

Any transaction requires either a medium of exchange or a contract *(or both)*. In the early days, these trades were fulfilled by an exchange of markers, **stones** or sticks in return for assets or services.

The recording of transactions is now being overtaken by **blockchain** technology that will ultimately transform commerce as we know it.

The tiny island of Yap, in the South Pacific, is unique in its use of ancient stone money, called the fei, as their currency for trade since 1400 AD. These huge limestone circular "coins", impossible to counterfeit, are still used on the island as its _trusted_ currency. They can be exchanged without actually being moved. The trust in their intrinsic value is immutable.

Bitcoin is "mined" using blockchain technology. The purpose of this book is to enlighten you about why Bitcoin and other cryptocurrencies are volatile and speculative while the technology upon which they are based, the blockchain, is a trusted and immutable distributed ledger.

I will take you on a journey from stones as currency, through the evolution of computers, and into a world where blockchain technology is disrupting commerce and, in the logistics industry, is requisite.

In this book, I explore the timeline and history of computing and artificial intelligence, along with technological breakthroughs that are disrupting commerce, transforming transactional processes, and eliminating middlemen. I fully expect that what is now considered a disruption will be commonplace in the near future.

Employment of blockchain technology would not be possible without the availability of vast data storage facilities, extremely fast computers for cryptocurrency mining, and the ability to simplify complex and fragmented processes within the logistics and supply chain industry. This is especially true for supporting the worldwide distribution and administration of the COVID-19 vaccine.

Chapter 1. Numbers and Computers
Counting

Where did counting begin? Artifacts more than 5,000 years old have been found, with notches on bones. Were these notations etched to count seasons, kills, or the number of children?

The origins of mathematics accompanied the evolution of social systems. Many, many social needs and human interactions required calculation and numbers. As society formed and organized, the need to express *quantity* and to count emerged.

When society emerged from hunting and gathering into an agrarian culture, there arose a need to account for surpluses. Counting probably began spontaneously and independently from place to place and tribe to tribe. Various number systems emerged, remarkably similar.

Hunters and Gatherers

The first civilized city emerged about 4,000 years ago. Ur, in southern Mesopotamia *(now Iraq)* was the first village, settled by the inhabitants of Sumeria. It was the principal center of worship.

When the ruins of Ur were found and excavated around 1850, thousands of cuneiform tablets were uncovered, revealing administrative and literary documents. This was the beginning of commerce and the recording of

The ruins of Ur

The City of Ur *(reconstruction)*

transactions.

The transition from counting with markers *(such as **stones** or sticks)* to counting with mechanical devices occurred over thousands of years. When society realized that accounting records were required, statistics were not only saved but also archived. Scientists came along and developed logic to "formularize" counting. Mathematics was invented because of the need to track *value*, and the first computer was born so that formulas and algorithms could be digitized. More recently, with the advent of artificial intelligence and machine learning, remote control of devices as well as robotics became ubiquitous.

Computing

Who first conceived the idea that someday computers would "think" in such a way that one could not distinguish a computer from a human? Perhaps it was Alan Turing.

Born in 1912, this British crypto-analyst, computer scientist and marathon runner conceived the **Turing Machine**, which was the first model of a general-purpose computer.

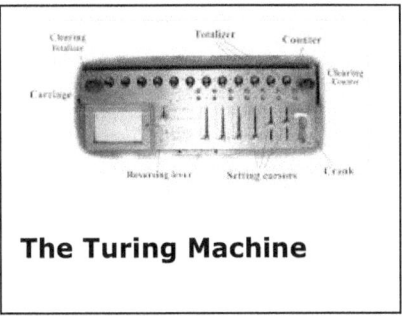

The Turing Machine

More germane to artificial intelligence was Turing's prediction that computers would someday "think" similarly to humans so that, if a problem were posed to a human in one room and a computer in another, the questioner could not distinguish from which room came the answer. Turing predicted that this would happen within 50 years with a 30% success rate. Although his prediction did not materialize, recent breakthroughs in artificial intelligence and machine learning have projected that, by **2030**, the 30% "indistinguishable" rate will be achieved.[1]

[1] Read another book by PAB, **2030-When Computers become Human**, on Amazon.com

Before 1810, little was known about "computing" other than the use of counting devices dating back to the ancient abacus. In 1804, Frances Jacquard developed a fully automated loom that was programmed by an early version of the punch card. By 1820, Charles Xavier Thomas de Colmar created the "**Arithometer**", the first commercially successful mechanical calculating machine, which remarkably could add, subtract, multiply and divide.

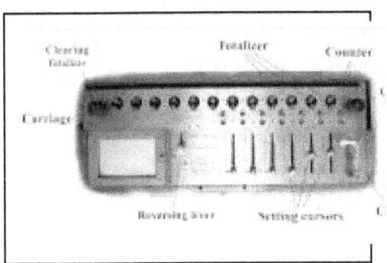

In parallel with the stages of development of the computer was the evolution of number systems. It all started when humans had reasons to count. Animals counted their young and birds deserted their nests when more than one egg was taken from them.

Ancient Incas, a highly advanced civilization, had no written language but developed the **Quipu** counting system, a system where thin strings were looped around a larger cord. It is believed that this was the *first* base-10 numbering system.

Ancient Egyptians had an understanding of fractions. They wrote fractions with a numerator of 1 but used hieroglyphics for the denominator. Their numbering system was a base-10 system with a unique sign for every power of 10.

The Babylonian system is one of the oldest systems, dating back 5,000 years. It was a system of wedge-shaped "tally" marks, and had a value depending upon the direction in which the wedge was pointing. It was also the first symbolic system used to tell the time of day.

The Mayan numbering system in the fourth century AD was perhaps a thousand times more advanced than the European system. Mayas used a Base-20 system which had only two symbols, a dot and a dash. They were the first to symbolize the concept of zero.

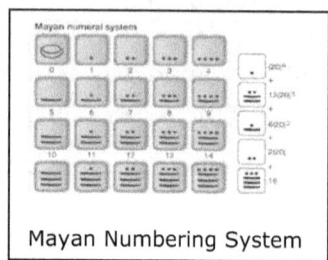

Mayan Numbering System

The Greek numbering system, interestingly enough, was based upon their own alphabet, which came from the Phoenicians.

The Roman numbering system, still used today, had a rather static numbering system which changed only slightly through time. It is perhaps best known in the United States for counting Super Bowls[2]. They are still used in almost all cases for the copyright date on films, television programs, and videos - for example, MCMLXXXVI for 1986. Roman numerals are also used to show the hours on some analog clocks and watches, and for numbering the preliminary pages of a book (i.e., I ii iii) before the main page numbering in the chapters begins. Monarchs (i.e., Popes and Kings) are usually designated with Roman numerals following their first name.

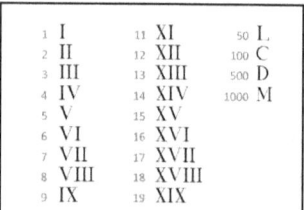

The base-10 decimal system is the most widely used system in the civilized world. Because it uses the digits 0 through 9 and powers of ten for the position of the digit in the number, it can represent any number, no matter how large. A shorthand for notating very large numbers is floating point.

---

[2] Except for Super Bowl **L**, which was called Super Bowl 50.

Early computer manufacturers realized that the decimal system does not lend itself to logical processes, nor could it easily be integrated on a computer's processor. The decimal system was replaced on computers with a base-2 **binary** system using only two symbols, 0 and 1, called "bits". It represents logic as well, since 1 is always true and 0 is always false.

All data and logic operations within a computer's memory or processor is stored as a series of zeros and ones. The position within a sequence of bits has a value based upon the power of 2.

For example, the four bits represented by "0111" has a decimal value of 14 (0+2+4+8). Arabic characters and numbers are represented in 8 bits, and can be displayed as a **hexadecimal** number represented by the digits **0-9** followed by the characters **A-F**. For example the character 15 in hexadecimal is stored in a computer as "**F**" which is "1111".

Used for programming, computer commands in low-level Assembly language are represented by two hexadecimal characters. For example, the *Branch on Condition* command is coded as "**FC**".

 **Charles Babbage** was born on December 26th, 1791, the son of a banker. He graduated from Cambridge University in 1810. He was known for his keen interest in mathematics and awesome expertise with calculus.

Often called "The Father of Computing," Babbage was an innovative thinker and a pioneer in the computing field. His knowledge of mathematics was so respected that he was hired by the Royal Institution shortly after graduation to lecture on calculus. Only two years later, he was elected a member of the Royal Society and along with some friends, founded the **Astronomical Society** in 1820.

By 1822, Babbage designed a "difference engine", which is a mechanical calculator that tabulates polynomials. The engine itself consisted of parallel tubular columns which were precisely machined to produce error-free calculations. The machine used the decimal numbering system and was manually powered by cranking a handle.

The British government became most interested in Babbage's engine, since producing tables of statistics at that time was time-consuming, expensive and not always 100% accurate.

In 1822, Babbage presented his "difference engine" to the Royal Astronomical Society in a paper entitled "Notes on the application of machinery to the computation of astronomical and mathematical tables." The British government gave Babbage £1700, a lot of pounds in those days, and work began on the project.

Babbage's goal was to overcome errors in tables with mechanization. Every part of the engine was formed by hand with custom machine tools, which Babbage himself constructed.

The result was an "engine" that was able to calculate polynomials by using a numerical method called "differences".

Logic

George Boole[3], born in 1815, was an English mathematician, philosopher and logician. He is considered to be the inventor of **Boolean Logic**, which is the foundation for the digital computer.

In 1849, Boole was appointed as the first professor of mathematics at Queens College in Ireland. His early works attempted to systematize the fundamental principles of Aristotle's logic.

Boole did not regard logic as a branch of mathematics. Instead, he proposed that logical propositions could be presented algebraically through the manipulation of symbols in equations.

The fundamental thesis for his logic consists of "elective symbols", primarily the logical operators "and" and "or" *(represented in formulas as "**&**" and "**|**")*. When coupled with a binary numbering system, this is the essence of Boolean logic in computer programming. Boole is considered to be the inventor of computer

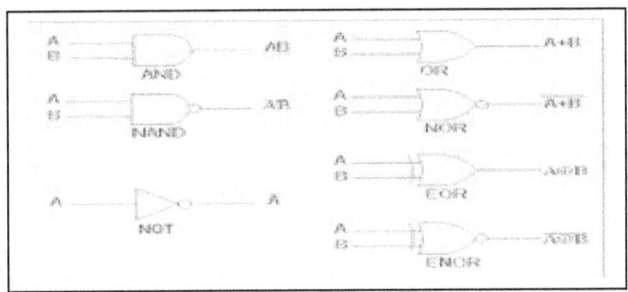

programming.

---

[3] Pete Bornstein was Director of Product Management at **Boole & Babbage** in Santa Clara, CA in the 80's.

Boole's contributions to the algebra of logic were viewed as immensely important and influential in the development of early computer processors. In early computers the Central Processing Unit (CPU) hosted algebraic logic, basic commands and mathematical operations, which was in essence a computer program integrated into the hardware of a computer. The first personal computers assembled all these components on a "motherboard", which hobbyists could modify.

Boole also conceived of the fundamental method of comparing "sets" by using just three operators: AND, OR and NOT.

His novel approach *(at the time)* of using only two symbols *(1 and 0)* to represent opposites is fundamental to programming logic. Tests of the symbols to mean "yes-no", "true-false" or "on-off" can result in "branches" to a portion of a computer program depending on whether it is a 1 or a 0. Furthermore, these tests can be nested within other tests and resolved from the inside out to produce a single "true" or "false". This is called "nested logic".

Boolean logic is the basic structure not only for computer programs but also for computer hardware, where "gates" on chips direct the flow through computer programs.

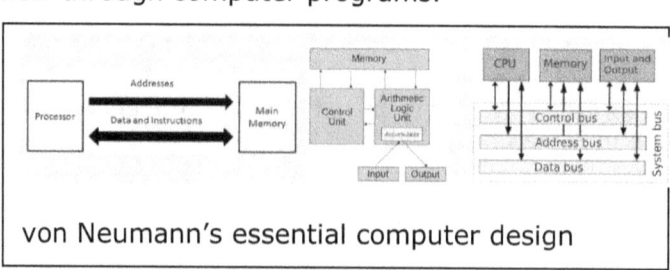

von Neumann's essential computer design

What is a "computer"? The fundamental architectural model for a computer was first described in June 1945, by **John von Neumann** and it survives today. The von Neumann model states that a computer's essential components are (1) a central processing unit *(CPU)*, (2) an arithmetical and logical component *(ALU)*, (3) mass storage, (4) a program "counter", and (5) input / output (I/O) channels. It was the "bible" for early computer engineers and designers.

In 1935, von Neumann introduced the concept of a stored program which could be input into a computer's random-access memory (RAM). Charles Babbage's Analytical Engine incorporated the von Neumann model and provided the ability to input programs from decks of punch cards. This concept was based upon the Jacquard loom of 1801.

von Neumann was probably the first to articulate the similarity between the computer and the brain. The output of neurons in the brain is essentially digital and sequential, while operating together as massively parallel processes. In the human brain, neural output is transmitted through axons, which is remarkably similar to an analog signal in processors.

Advances in technology continue to significantly increase computer processing speeds and will ultimately achieve the "singularity[4]" between brains and computers.

---

[4] Read Ray Kurzweil's The Singularity is Near (2005).

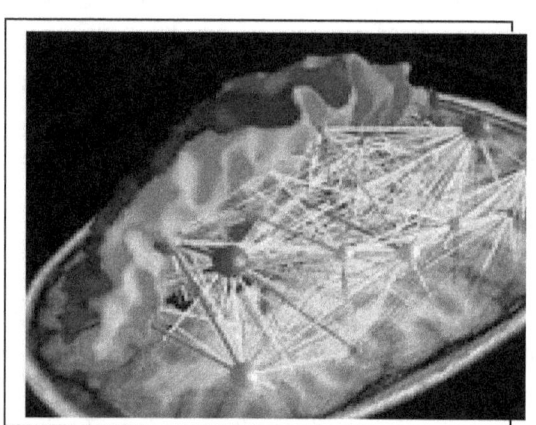

Punch Cards

Throughout history, civilized man had a need to record information. The first evidence of the use of the number 1 seems to be about 20,000 years ago, when a uniform series of single lines cut into the "Ishanga" bone *(the fibula of a baboon)*, was discovered by archaeologists. It represented numbers by a series of ones.

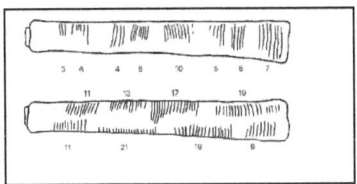

Numbers and counting didn't come into extensive use until the rise of cities and commerce, starting around 4000 BC. When subtraction was joined with addition, arithmetic was born.

Evidence of recording devices first appeared in the form of clay cones gathered in clay pouches. Later these cones were replaced by marks on clay tablets. Ancient Sumerians recognized the need for people to keep track of material possessions and the accounting industry was born.

Around 3000 BC, the number 1 was transformed from a counting unit to a unit of measurement, employed to measure length. Builders of temples and pyramids invented the cubit, which was probably the first standardized unit of measure. The cubit was an ancient measure of length, approximately equal to the length of a male forearm. It was typically about 18 inches or 44 cm, though there was a *long cubit* of about 21 inches or 52 cm.

Under the guidance of Pythagoras, the Greeks developed the concept of odd and even numbers. Later, another Greek mathematician Archimedes formulated theoretical math, and his experiments with mathematics within *games* led to practical application in the world of commerce and banking.

While counting and calculating with numbers, there arose a need to store the results so that they could be recalled later and analyzed by accountants, researchers, or census bureaus. Politicians needed to know how many constituents were in their district, and whether they were red or blue *(or Tea Party)*.

The earliest medium for data storage in early PCs was in the form of "punch cards" containing, at first, round holes, and later, rectangular holes[5]. One of the early uses for round-hole punch cards was for toll tickets on east coast turnpikes, to record where the vehicle entered and then to charge the proper toll upon exit.

> **The First Industrial Revolution**
>
> The first industrial revolution spans from the end of the 18th century to the beginning of the 19th century. It witnessed the emergence of **mechanization**, a process that replaced agriculture with industry as the foundation for the economic structure of society.

As early as 1725, cards with round holes were

---
[5] These rectangular holes frequentlyhad hanging chads, made infamo[us during the] election recount in Florida.

used for controlling textile looms. In 1890, **Herman Hollerith** designed and developed the first punch card machine after contracting with the federal government to process the results of the 1880 census. His design was based upon the Jacquard loom[6], and the operational system was completed in just three years.

Hollerith's machine saved the US government five million dollars, a good part of the total budget at that time. Hollerith later formed a company which today is known as IBM.

The punch card machine was created at the very beginning of the 1st Industrial Revolution. Interestingly, the 60 million cards punched in the 1890 census *(presumably one per person in the United States)* were fed *manually* into this machine. The counts for each column were displayed in dials on the face of the tabulator. A "demographic recorder" attached to the machine would be activated by certain hole combinations, resulting in a set of statistics *(i.e., the number of married men over 50 with fulltime jobs)*.

The remarkable growth of IBM in its early years is attributable in great part to the "IBM card", as the punch card came to be known. In IBM's first 50 years, the data on punch cards held nearly all of the world's collected data.

IBM's Punch Card

---

[6] Jacquard also influenced Charles Babbage, who used punch cards to control the sequence of computations in his analytical engine.

Punch cards were the foundation of early mainframe computers, and for IBM, extremely profitable.

In 1928, IBM transformed and standardized the punch card to be the exact size of a dollar bill, with rectangular holes and 80 columns, some of which could be used as sequence numbers after very tired programmers on the night shift *(like me)* dropped their decks.

A cottage industry was born. These "service bureaus" employed clerks who performed data entry and tabulation.

Television

With "engines" now computing and making decisions, along with media input and printer output, a missing components for a complete "personal" computer were a display *(or monitor)* and later, a mouse.

In June 2014, I was privileged to spend an evening with **Phil Savenick** at his sprawling home in Westwood, California, next door to UCLA. Phil is a former Disney animation executive, filmmaker, artist and historian, with a fascinating knowledge of the evolution of television.

At the center of Phil's home is a museum dedicated to television history, and a shrine to **Philo Farnsworth**, the pioneer of the technology that made modern television possible.

Farnsworth, born in 1906, was raised in a poor home with no electricity. In 1919, his family moved to his Uncle Albert's 240-acre ranch near Rigby, Idaho, to sharecrop. Fortunately, the ranch not only had electricity but also a cache of science magazines like **Popular Science** in the attic, which Philo read avidly.

Phil Savenick with Philo Farnsworth's farrow tool

Philo's thirst for knowledge opened a whole world of creativity and inventiveness. One day, while driving a farm vehicle, Philo looked at the newly plowed field, and what he saw was evenly parallel lines, in row after row. It occurred to him that an image could be sliced into rows, back and forth, and each row could be transmitted in a continuous sequence. **Raster imaging** was born.

At age 14, Philo used a lens to direct light into a glass camera tube, inventing what would later be called a

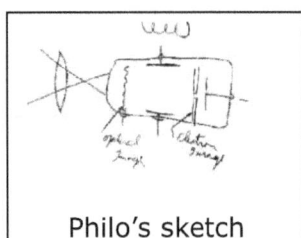

Philo's sketch

vacuum tube. In his chemistry class in Rigby, Idaho, Farnsworth sketched out his "camera" tube.

Although neither his teacher nor his fellow students grasped the implications of this concept, he had created the fundamental architecture that would revolutionize television.

Farnsworth's first Vacuum Tube.   The first televisions. 7

In 1926, Farnsworth scraped together enough funds to continue his scientific work and he moved to San Francisco with his new wife, Elma "Pem" Gardner Farnsworth.

The following year, he took a glass slide, smoked it with carbon and scratched a single line on it. This was placed in a carbon arc projector and shone on to the photocathode of his vacuum tube. He then unveiled his all-electronic television prototype - the first of its kind - made possible by a video camera tube or "image dissector."

Between 1926 and 1929, Farnsworth was consumed by a lengthy legal battle with RCA and other corporate giants, who claimed that *they* had first invented the cathode ray tube (CRT). He won the case in court, his most convincing evidence being the sketch of his vacuum tube *(on the previous page)*.

[7] In Phil Savenick's museum of television history

Farnsworth was granted Patent #1,773,981 on August 25, 1930, for his CRT. This first emerged as a display tube for all black and white television screens in the early days of television, and he began to receive royalties from RCA and other manufacturers.

In 1930, his wife, "Pem" Farnsworth became the first television actress. In early television filming, she could not face the camera directly because the lights were so hot. She was required to move away completely after only a few moments.

Pem Farnsworth – the first TV Star.

By the age of 64, Farnsworth held more than 300 United States and foreign patents, most of which formed the foundation of the television industry as it swept the world and changed the nature of modern civilization and communications.

Early Computers

The earliest calculators were mechanical, controlled by push-buttons or levers. They were driven by gears, cams, belts or shafts.

The second industrial revolution brought the emergence of new sources of energy. Computers could now be powered by electricity.

> **The Second Industrial Revolution**
>
> At the end of the 19th century, technological advancements witnessed the emergence of a new source of energy: electricity, gas and oil. This led to the development of the combustion engine, which used these resources to their full potential. Communications was revolutionized with the invention of the telegraph and the telephone, and the automobile and the plane witnessed widespread consumer use.

ABC Computer

In 1937, **J.V. Atanasoff**, a professor of physics and mathematics at Iowa State University, built the first non-mechanical computer, called the Atanasoff-Berry (ABC) computer. It was the first electric-powered digital computer.

By 1941, Atanasoff and his graduate student, Clifford Berry, created the first "multi-tasking" computer that could solve up to 29 equations simultaneously.

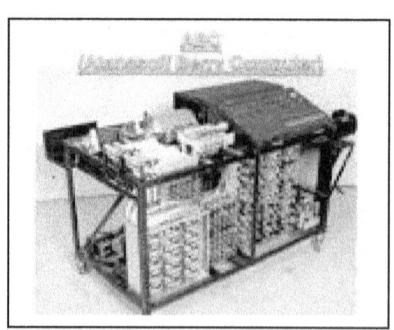

The **Atanasoff-Berry** computer is sometimes credited as being the first to store programs in its main memory. However, these "programs" were actually hard-coded solutions to linear equations.

There is some debate about whether the "Berry" was really the first *digital* computer. Some computer historians give this accolade to **John Mauchly** and **Presper Eckert**, creators of the **ENIAC**[8] computer, discussed in the next chapter [Mainframes].

---

[8] See http://www.computerhistory.org/revolution/birth-of-the-computer/4/78

Other noteworthy developments in computing technology:

In 1937, **George Stibitz** of Bell Labs constructed a 1-bit binary "adder", which was one of the first binary computers.

In 1940, also at Bell Labs, Stibitz and **Samuel Williams** built a "Model I Relay Calculator", which could operate on complex numbers.

In 1941, developers at the German Aeronautical Research Institute completed the first operational programmable calculator, which supported floating point[9] numbers.

1n 1943, a team *(that included Turing)* at the Government Code and Cypher School in England completed a machine dedicated to cipher-breaking, the first decryption machine used in World War II. The same team also developed a programmable calculator, where both programs and data were read in from paper tapes.

---

[9] The term **floating point** is derived from the fact that there is no fixed number of digits before and after the decimal point; that is, the decimal point can float. Significant digits are scaled using an exponent to a fixed base (i.e., 10^5 or 10^{-6}).

Mainframes

The earliest computers, called "mainframes", were designed and developed by pioneers in computing.

ENIAC

In 1944, the first electronic computer arrived. It was the *Electronic Numerical Integrator and Calculator* (**ENIAC**), financed by the U.S. Army and designed by two University of Pennsylvania professors, **John Mauchly** and J. **Presper Eckert**.

Because of its size, the ENIAC is recognized as the father of mainframe digital computers. It filled a 20x40 foot room and had 18,000 vacuum tubes. It was capable of being reprogrammed to solve a broad array of numerical problems.

The ENIAC was initially designed for the Army and was employed to calculate artillery firing tables based upon the ballistics of weapons at that time. The media portrayed it as "a Giant Brain", with a breakthrough speed *(at that time)*, of 1,000 times that of electro-mechanical machines.

Shortly after the end of World War II, the ENIAC was programmed to analyze the feasibility of developing the hydrogen bomb.

UNIVAC

In 1946, Mauchly and Eckert left the University of Pennsylvania and received funding from the Census Bureau to build the **UNIVAC**, the first commercial computer for business and government data processing.

The increasing demand for large computers was triggered when "second generation" transistors[10] replaced vacuum-tubes in the late 1950s. This spurred development in hardware and software, but early manufacturers usually built small quantities of each model, targeting them to a narrowly defined vertical market. They were not sold to the general public.

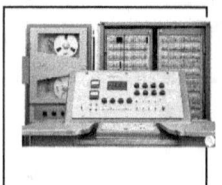
The **NEAC 2203** computer was one of the first *transistorized* computers. It was developed in Japan in 1960 for the purpose of managing Japan's Kinki Nippon Railways online reservation system.

The NEAC supported both Roman and Japanese character sets, and may have been the world's first multilingual computer.

IBM was a pioneer of advancements in the power and capability of mainframes in the fifties and sixties. The first automatic digital calculator in the United States, built for Harvard University in 1944, was named the **Automatic Sequence Controlled Calculator**.

Other significant computers in the IBM chronology:

1946: the **IBM 603** Electronic Multiplier, the first calculator to be placed in production.

1948: the successful **IBM 604** Electronic Calculating Punch.

1949: the Card Programmable Calculator (**CPC**), the first IBM product designed specifically for use in data service centers.

1952: the **IBM 701**, the company's first commercially available scientific computer.

---

[10] Transistors were first used in handheld calculators.

1953: the **IBM 650** Magnetic Drum Calculator, the largest selling computer in the 1950s, and the **IBM 702** Electronic Data Processing Machine, with data and programs stored on tape drives.

1954: the Naval Ordnance Research Calculator (**NORC**), for many years the fastest computer in the World.

1956: the **SAGE** (Semi-Automatic Ground Environment) AN/FSQ-7 series of computers, used for a quarter-century in the U.S. air defense system.

1957: the **IBM 305** Random Access Memory Accounting Machine (**RAMAC**), which employed a magnetic disk memory unit for real-time "in-line data processing".

IBM's "big iron" Data Processing Division (DPD) was formed in 1956 to focus on the design, manufacturing, distribution and marketing of mainframe computers for commercial use:

1958: the **IBM 7090**, which hosted the first networked commercial airline reservation system, the proprietary **SABRE** software. It later was used by NASA to control the Mercury and Gemini space flights. The 7090 was a solid-state fully transistorized system with computer speeds six times that of its vacuum-tube predecessor, the **IBM 709**.

1960: the **IBM 7030 STRETCH** computer, the most powerful and versatile computer in the world at that time. The first 7030 was manufactured for the Los Alamos Scientific Laboratory under contract to the Atomic Energy Commission. The 7030 computers featured unrivaled speed, memory capacity, input-output flexibility, and multiprogramming capability.

As mainframes became smaller in size and faster, they eventually gave way to "mini-computers" and word processing machines that could serve the needs of small businesses. These machines usually cost less than $25,000 and were capable of running high-level programs like Fortran *(see next section)*.

Programming

Ada Lovelace, the daughter of Lord Byron *(Lovelace)*, was born in 1815 and is considered to be the world's first programmer. She had a passion for technology and mathematics.

Although she married an aristocrat, William Lord King, her true soulmate was **Charles Babbage**. Although Babbage is given credit for inventing the **Difference Engine** and later, the **Analytical Engine**, he was exasperated that the logarithm tables hardcoded within these engines were fraught with errors and could not be relied upon by navigators, astronomers and bankers.

Ada enlightened a frustrated Babbage with "Ada's Algorithm", which postulated that his Analytical Engine could be applied to *any* process that manipulated data. Her translation of data into a *process* stored within an "engine" was truly the first programming language.

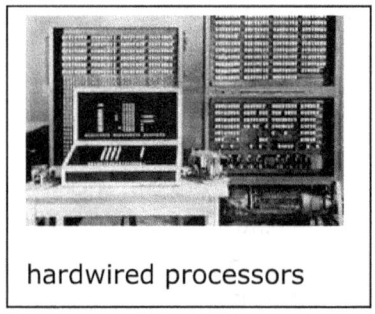

hardwired processors

Between 1977 and 1983, a programming language named **Ada** was developed by a team led by Jean Ichbiah of Honeywell Bull under contract to the U S Dept. of Defense. Ada superseded over 450 programming languages used by the DoD at that time and became the DOD programming standard. By 1985, this standard was replaced by C, C++ and then Java.

Unfortunately, Ada Lovelace never received any remuneration for her algorithm, and only used income derived from Ada to bet on horses. She ran up huge gambling debts and died relatively unknown at age 36 of uterine cancer.

Ada's algorithmic concept led to the development of early programming "languages" such as **Plan Calculus** in 1945. These programs were hard-wired into computers and controlled by toggle switches on the computer's panel.

As mainframes became more widely used in most industries, the need arose for mid-size and large enterprises in commerce and government to rely on in-house computer programming staffs. Resources for designing and developing programs for general purpose computers were in short supply, and early programming languages were low-level, employing constructs of ones and zeros *(bits)* as computer coded instructions.

Assembly language, first created for the **EDSAC** computer in 1949, was one of the first low-level binary programming languages where programs were fed into mainframe computers on punch cards or magnetic tape. Usually, a single program would run on a mainframe computer that was not capable of multi-tasking.

Programs written with low-level Assembly instructions were then converted to executable machine instructions by utility software tools called Assemblers.

Because of the need to write commercial programs at a much higher coding level, early programming language developers recognized the need for English-like languages.

Grace Hopper led a team at Remington Rand in 1959 that developed **COBOL**[11], the first commercial high-level programming

---

[11] **COBOL** stands for Common Business Oriented Language.

language. It was the first "user-friendly" and intuitive business-oriented programming language.

Once COBOL programs were entered into computers via data entry devices *(punchcard readers),* they were stored on media and then compiled and converted into machine language. A single COBOL instruction would expand to hundreds of machine instructions in the computer.

Examples of COBOL instructions:

```
MOVE EMPLOYEE_FULL_NAME TO EMPLOYEE-NAME
COMPUTE ANNUAL-SALARY = MONTHLY * 12
PERFORM 2500-PROCESS-EMPLOYEES UNTIL END-OF-FILE[12]
IF MONTHLY-SALARY > 4000
PERFORM 3000-SALARIED-EMPLOYEES
ELSE
PERFORM 3100-HOURLY-EMPLOYEES
END-IF
END.
```

Almost immediately, COBOL standards were established by the American National Standards Institute (ANSI) to ensure that input to compilers on any mainframe computer was consistent, while output of the compiler depended upon its developer and design.

COBOL was designed for the development of business applications, and typically processed files on tape drives, or on large portable disk drives. Later, as database systems such as IMS or DB2 were developed, COBOL was enhanced to process hierarchical or relational databases instead of "flat" files.

A fault in the language not realized until the 1990s was that many COBOL programs were written to store the year as a two-digit number *(i.e., "96").* As a result, most large companies scrambled during the 1990s to hire "Y2K" teams[13] to convert all programs and data to use 4-digit years. The teams were so successful that

---

[13] Pete was on Chevron's team in 1999.

the predicted doomsday on 1/1/2000 never occurred.

In the late 1940s and early 1950s, John Backus at IBM assembled and guided a team of young men and women with a specific goal - to develop a programming language that could solve mathematical problems. His team consisted on a cryptographer, a chess wizard, programmers, mathematicians and engineers. Backus **recognized that mathematicians and scientists required a more algebraic and formula-oriented programming language, and FORTRAN**[14] was born.

FORTRAN was designed for iterative logical or mathematical processes, or "Loops", that continued until an intended result, or a series on repetitive results, was achieved[15].

In 1975, Backus was awarded the National Medal of Science, and two years later, the prestigious Turing Award.

Examples of FORTRAN statements:

```
SUBROUTINE SUB1(X,DUMSUB)
INTEGER N, X
EXTERNAL DUMSUB
COMMON /GLOBALS/ N
IF(X .LT. N)THEN
X = X + 1
PRINT *, 'x = ', X
CALL DUMSUB(X,DUMSUB)
END IF
END
```

---

[14] **FOR**mula **TRAN**slator
[15] One flaw in this concept was that if the intended result was never achieved, this became the dreaded "infinite loop".

In 1965, The **PL/1** programming language was released to the public by IBM. PL/1 was developed by IBM at its Hursley, England development lab and was used internally at IBM for manufacturing systems[16].

PL/1 brought to programmers a combination of COBOL's business-programming capabilities and FORTRAN's mathematical and scientific functions. Like COBOL, it is procedural and English-like. Like FORTRAN, it can be used for numerical computation, scientific computing and even systems programming.

One of PL/1's unique strengths was bit and character string manipulation. It has many powerful "Built-in" pre-coded functions for repetitive processes which can be invoked from within a main program, thus reducing coding time considerably.

Examples of PL/1 statements:

```
DCL ALPHABET CHAR(26) INIT('ABC');
DCL BIN_NUMBER FIXED BIN(31) INIT(99);
DCL PIC_NUMBER PIC'99V.99' INIT(99.9);
IF (GTO_DELTA=5) & (RETURN_TO_DEPART='N') THEN PUT
LIST('RETURN= '||ORIG_DTE||' '||ORIG_TIM||' '||APPL_KVL);
IF THIS_IS_TRUE = YES
THEN CALL YOU_ARE_RIGHT;
ELSE CALL YOU_ARE_WRONG;
```

The most widely used object-oriented programming language available for programming web pages in the early days of the internet was **Java**. Java combined snippets of code (*Objects*) into interactive web pages. Java was reliable and employed dynamic run-time error checking. However, it was not secure.

Today, the most widely used web development languages are **HTML**, a standardized markup language; **CSS**, a style-sheet language; **JavaScript**, widely used for animation and interactive games; **ActionScript**, used with Adobe Flash; **PHP**, used by web servers; and **Python**, a general-purpose programming language.

---

[16] Pete headed up a project developing an internal system to manage unit assemblies before PL/1 was released to the public.

Chips

The 3rd industrial revolution brought integrated electronics components into computers.

> **The Third Industrial Revolution**
>
> The third industrial revolution arrived in the early 1970s with the emergence of nuclear energy. This revolution also witnessed the rise of electronics, with the transistor and microprocessor, and also the broad use of telecommunications via satellites.

The development of faster and significantly smaller computers advanced remarkably in the fifties. A major trigger for these technological advances was the replacement of vacuum tubes with transistors.

The type of vacuum tube used in early televisions and computers was the triode, invented by **Lee de Forest** in 1906. It was comprised of a cathode and a plate, separated by a control grid, and suspended in a glass vacuum tube.

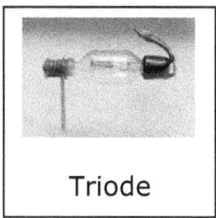
Triode

The control grid manages the flow of electrons in either direction. By making it negative, electrons are repelled back to the cathode. When positive, electrons are attracted to the plate.

The control grid was an effective on-off switch, but it consumed excessive power and gave off tremendous heat. These tubes failed often in large computers and were unreliable.

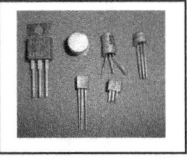
Tubes were ultimately replaced by transistors, a transformational contribution to the evolution of the computer in the 50's through the 70's. Invented in 1947 at Bell Laboratories, it was a reliable solid-

state electronic switch, considerably smaller than the vacuum tube, which produced little heat.

In 1948, Bell associate **William Shockley** invented the bipolar junction transistor (BJT), which relied on two types of semiconductors for its operation. BJTs can be used as amplifiers, switches or oscillators *(for timing)*.

Many BJTs were combined in large numbers on the first integrated circuits, invented in 1958 by **Jack Kilby** and **Robert Noyce**. Integrated circuits later came to be known as computer "chips" because they are built on a slice of silicon.

In 1964, **Douglas Engelbart** demonstrated a prototype of the modern computer, with a mouse and a simple graphical user interface **(GUI),** with a "motherboard" populated with integrated circuits. This signaled the transition of the computer from a specialized machine for scientists and mathematicians, to those that were more accessible and user-friendly for the general public.

In 1970, the newly formed **Intel** unveiled the Intel 1103, utilizing *dynamic random-access memory* **(DRAM)** chips as PC processors. DRAMs allow the processor to access any location in memory directly rather than having to proceed sequentially from a starting point.

At this point, the world was ready for personal computers.
- 1977 brought about a "Trinity" of successful commercial computers, comprised of the Apple II, the Commodore PET and Radio Shacks TRS-80.
- In 1981, IBM launched its Personal Computer intended for interactive individual use.
- The Apple Lisa and the Macintosh became immensely popular in the 80s because of their user-friendly graphic user interface, driven by a mouse and a keyboard.
- The 1990s and early 2000s brought much increased performance and data storage to the PC, with IBMs ThinkPad, Dell's PC, Hewlett-Packard PCs and others.

Moore's Law

Gordon Moore was born in San Francisco in 1929. He received a B.S. in chemistry from Cal Berkeley in 1950, and a Ph.D. in chemistry and physics from Caltech in 1954. He conducted post-doctoral research at Johns Hopkins University from 1953 to 1956.

Gordon Moore

Moore was the co-founder *(along with* **Robert Noyce***)* and ultimately chairman emeritus of Intel Corporation. In 1971, his net worth was estimated to be over $8 billion.

Before founding Intel, Moore worked as Director of R&D at Fairchild Semiconductor. In 1965, in an interview by Electronics Magazine, he stated *that the* **number of transistors in a dense integrated circuit doubles every year, at a constant price point**, *and would continue to do so for the next 10 years.* In 1975, he lengthened his predicted forecast rate to every *two* years.

This forecast, called **Moore's law**, established a paradigm in the semiconductor industry for reducing chip size while holding to the same price point. His prediction proved to be quite accurate well into the late 80's.

Moore's law continues to be a measuring stick in the semi-conductor industry for long-term planning and for setting targets and goals for research and development. Since 1961, the number of transistors on a chip actually doubled every 18 months at the same price point until 2011.

Interestingly, the law held over all these years because transistors have an inherent quality of performing better as they get smaller. This means that more and more transistors can be used on devices without requiring more power or generating excessive heat. However, as they get smaller, they become less efficient, the cost of manufacturing rises, and they approach a fundamental limit of smallness. Slowing increases in revenue and large increases in cost seem to indicate that Moore's Law finally suffered its demise in 2011.

Personal Computers

In the late 1960's a niche market for PCs was created primarily by hobbyists and sold mostly within their own interest groups. Many of these early PCs were sold as kits and had to be assembled by their buyers. Pioneers in this initial entry into the personal computer world included:

- In 1974, the **Altair 8800** was featured on the cover of Popular Electronics and sold only by mail order through advertisements in hobbyist magazines. It is recognized as the world's first commercially successful personal computer.
- In 1975, the **IBM 5100** became the first commercially available "portable" computer.
- In 1976, Steve Jobs and Steve Wozniak founded Apple Computers in a garage and rolled out the **Apple I**, the first personal computer with a single circuit board.
- In 1977, Radio Shack's initial production run of the **TRS-80** *(affectionately called the Trash-80)* was just 3,000. With a handle and a carrying case, it sold out almost immediately.
- Also in 1977, the **Commodore PET** became a top seller in the educational market and is considered to be the first "all-in-one" personal computer, with a keyboard and a monitor.

The first *mass-marketed* personal computer was launched by IBM in 1981. Code named **Acorn**, it used Microsoft's MS-DOS operating system. It had an Intel chip, two floppy disks and an optional color monitor. It was sold at Sears and Computerland, marking the first time that personal computers were sold at retail through outside distributors.

In 1983, Apple introduced the **Lisa**[17] computer, the first PC with a graphical user interface (GUI). This was followed in 1984 by the **Macintosh**, which not only had an improved GUI[18] but was also the first successful mouse-driven computer.

[17] LISA stood for "Local Integrated Software Architecture, but it was also the name of Steve Job's daughter.

In 1986, Compaq offered the **Deskpro 386**, with processing speed comparable to mainframes at that time, using 32-bit[19] architecture.

IBM's **PS/2** computer, introduced in 1987, featured a 3-1/2" floppy drive and VGA monitor, which became industry standards for most early personal computers.

---

[18] Graphic User Interface
[19] "bit" architecture is the number of bits (0s and 1s) within a single computer's low-level "machine" instruction.

Chapter 2. Artificial Intelligence

The Turing Test

When will a computer become human? In 1951, the British mathematician Alan Turing postulated that, if a person were in one room and a computer in another room, if a "judge" could not determine from which room the response to his questions came, *artificial intelligence* could not be distinguished from human intelligence.

The movie about Turing's theory, called **The Imitation Game** was released in 2014. The movie portrays the life of Turing, starring Benedict Cumberbatch as Turing, and Keira Knightley as Joan Clark, his star crypto-analyst.

Artificial intelligence (**AI**) is anything a device[20] can do that was formerly considered to be a task for a human being.

---

[20] What was referred to earlier as a "computer" or a "machine" will be called a "device" for the remainder of this book.

Research

Early research into artificial intelligence was highly technical and specialized, focusing on accomplishing a *specific* outcome. Initial applications attempted to emulate human thinking programmatically with "if-then-else" rules, but this approach failed because of the vast number of possibilities that needed to be applied to a specific task. Researchers were much more successful when the technology was applied through a device that perceives its environment through sensors and makes decisions or takes actions based upon ever-increasing machine learning accumulated in the device's knowledge base. This concept was introduced commercially in 1990 at the Massachusetts Institute of Technology (MIT) and first found its way into homes as the Roomba vacuum cleaner[21].

Goals in AI research continue to focus on reasoning, machine learning, development of knowledge bases, design and planning, natural language processing, perception, and the ability to manipulate objects. This field is predicated upon the goal that intelligence can be so precisely emulated in a machine that a device will eventually emulate a human. This raises the ethical concern that we might be creating artificial beings endowed with human characteristics.

Greek mythology envisioned "thinking machines" such as the bronze robot of Hephaestus, and Pygmalion's Galatea. Every major civilization believed in some sort of human likeness endowed with intelligence. By the 20th century, artificial beings were introduced in fiction, such as in Shelley's **Frankenstein**.

In the summer of 1956, academic research in AI originated at a conference in Dartmouth College. Dartmouth was the leader in AI research for several decades. By the mid-sixties, AI research in the United States was heavily funded by the Department of Defense.

---

[21] This was probably the world's first robot to be used as an appliance.

Although research into AI in the late fifties focused on *imitating* human intelligence, philosopher and logician **Noam Chomsky** and others at MIT explored cognitive science, a field aimed at *understanding* the mental form and rules that are the foundation of perceptual and cognitive abilities. Chomsky's work has influenced research not only in AI, but also in the fields of cognitive science, music theory, political science and programming language theory.

In 1979, exploration of AI emerged as a nonprofit society called the *Association for the Advancement of Artificial Intelligence* (**AAAI**). This society focuses on advancing the understanding of the mechanisms that underlie thought and intelligent behavior, and how this behavior can be embodied in machines.

Like most AI societies, AAAI is partially funded by member dues, donations and grants. AAAI organizes conferences, symposia and workshops and publishes a quarterly magazine for its members.

The term Artificial Intelligence is believed to have been coined in 1956 by **John McCarthy**[22] when he assembled the first academic conference on the subject at Stanford.

Researchers at Stanford focused on applied mathematical logic in computer programs to support the concept of AI. McCarthy was a leader of development teams that built early business programming languages such as LISP and ALGOL. In 1960, LISP was the programming language of choice for AI applications. Today's top programming languages for AI applications, in order of popularity, are Python, R, Lisp, Prolog and Java.

---

[22] McCarthy's license plate frame read *"Do the arithmetic or be doomed to talk nonsense"*.

No one has ever disputed a device's ability to process logic and produce an accurate result. However, most people question whether a machine can actually *think*. For this to happen, the machine must learn, and this is where *machine learning* and knowledge bases come into play.

Significant advances have been made in AI over the past 60 years, particularly with search algorithms *(i.e., Google)*, machine learning and the mass integration of statistical analysis within huge, distributed knowledge bases that are used to better understand society and human interaction.

Machine learning algorithms soon became imbedded in neural networks, modeled on how the human brain's neurons work. This concept was applied to a large body of knowledge, particularly to images. Social media sites, security apps and mass social monitoring *(think China)* apply this concept to facial recognition.

AI expectations continue to outpace reality. Significant breakthroughs have been promised *"in the next ten years"* for the past sixty years. After decades of research, no computer has come close to passing the Turing test, but with significant advances in voice recognition, we are getting close. Remarkably, IBM's **Watson** consistently wins at chess when playing against masters. Research in AI was encouraged by the Loebner Prize in 1995 and the associated Turing Test Competition, with a $100,000 reward for development of a system indistinguishable from a human.

Applying Artificial Intelligence

In an effort to construct a computer that could win a game of chess against a *master*, two approaches were used initially: **Type-A programs**, which would use pure brute force, examine thousands of moves *(permutations and combinations),* while employing a min/max search algorithm to specify the next move; or **Type-B programs**, which would use specialized heuristics and 'strategic' AI, examining only a few, key candidate moves that surfaced in a knowledge base.

The Type-A brute approach was successful in May 1997 when an IBM computer called **Deep Blue®** beat world chess champion Garry Kasparov after a six-game match: two wins for IBM, one for the champion and three draws.

Today, Type-A brute force programs are chosen over Type-B due to the exponentially increasing processing power of computer chips and *massively parallel* super-computers like Watson, along with the availability of vast data storage facilities with accumulated machine learning and processing with high-speed internet connections[23].

---

[23] The next frontier for Type-A programs will be to win at the ancient Asian game of **Go**. Whereas chess has a branching factor *(possible moves)* of 40, Go's branching factor approaches 200.

Expert systems, a subset of AI, attempt to model human expertise in *specific* knowledge areas. These systems have three components:

- A cumulative knowledge base
- An inference engine to process input
- An input/output (I/O) interface to interact with the user.

Expert systems are characterized by:

- The use of symbolic logic rather than numeric calculations
- Data-driven processing
- A knowledge base continually expanding through machine learning
- Ability of the user to interpret the systems' actions in a manner that is understandable and useful.

The dreams of scientists and science fiction go far beyond artificial intelligence and we are currently witnessing remarkable breakthroughs. The ultimate goal seems to be autonomous "thinking" systems that are free of human guidance or interference[24] such as self-driving vehicles. We are now at a point where devices provide spontaneous and unsolicited advice, knowledge, and guidance for their human "masters". Professionals in the eighties called these devices "personal assistants", but we have come a long way from that designation.

---

[24] Examples are: **Semi**-autonomous vehicles which take over safety actions for the driver, and drones used as first responders to disasters.

Robotics

Archytas Pigeon

Was a mechanical bird the first robot? Back in 350 B.C., Greek mathematician **Archytas** built a steam-powered clay "Pigeon" that was history's earliest study of flight, and probably the first model airplane.

Along came Greek philosopher **Aristotle**, born in 384 BC, who first conceived of "moral" robots as inanimate instruments that could do their own work, "at the word of command or by intelligent anticipation."

Robotic Knight

Move forward to 1495, when **Leonardo Da Vinci** built a mechanical device that looked like an armored knight. The mechanisms inside, mostly gears, weights and pulleys, were designed to amuse royalty and move like a human.

By 1770, Swiss clock makers, led by the inventor of the modern wristwatch, **Pierre Jaquet-Droz,** created three dolls to entertain royalty, one that could write, another that played music, and a third that drew pictures.

In 1898, **Nikola Tesla** *(does that name ring a bell?)* built and demonstrated a remote-controlled robotic boat at Madison Square Garden. Did he ever dream that a successor robotic vehicle would someday be powered by batteries or the sun?

Now let's look at the evolution of the today's robots with built-in machine learning and artificial intelligence.

The person credited with introducing the word "**Robot**" in 1921 was Czech writer **Karel Capek** in his play **R.U.R.** *(Rossum's Universal Robots)*. The Czech word "robota" means "compulsory labor".

In 1940, **Isaac Asimov** began to write a series of short stories about robots. The first was named **A Strange Playfellow** *(later* renamed *"Robbie")*. In 1950, all of his short stories were compiled into a single volume **I, Robot**.

Asimov's most important contribution to the field of robotics was his **Three Laws of Robotics**:

> 1. A robot may not injure a human being or, through inaction, allow a human being to come to harm.
> 2. A robot must obey the orders given by human beings except where such orders would conflict with the First Law.
> 3. A robot must protect its own existence as long as such protection does not conflict with the First Law or Second Law.

The employment of the third law, while ignoring laws 1 and 2, is demonstrated by **Hal** in "**2001-A Space Odyssey**".

In the 20th century, robotic technology advanced rapidly. Today, robots can assemble other machines more capable than themselves, and some robots are even mistaken for human beings *(observe greeters at Loews)*.

The robot in the mid-20th century was seen as a curiosity, even appearing on the **Tonight Show** in 1966. Before long, robots found a place in industrial manufacturing and spread rapidly to Japan, South Korea and throughout Europe. In the mid-sixties, the first operational industrial robot in North America was employed in a candy factory in Kitchener, Ontario.

Robotics has advanced dramatically in the 21st century for automating warehouses to fulfill orders and optimize logistics. Amazon is by far the leader in this application of robotics.

Robots have found a place in other vertical markets, such as toys and entertainment, military weapons, and search and rescue. Some even became "self-repairing" such as **W. Grey Walter's** Elmer and Elsie *(aka "turtle robots")*, who found their charging station when their batteries were low *(1948)*.

A major milestone in force feedback *(haptic[25])* technology were ray-based haptic-rendering algorithms that enabled the user to touch and feel convex polyhedral objects with a line segment model of a probe, first employed as a tele-operated articulated arm in 1951.

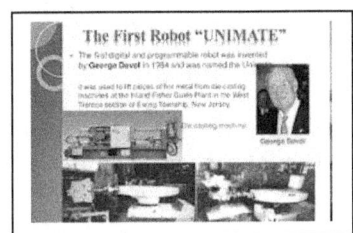

George Devol and **Joseph Engelberger**, in 1954, are credited with designing the first *truly* programmable robot. Named UNIMATE, it became the launch product for their company, **Unimation** Inc., believed to be the first company to manufacture and market robots for personal and commercial use. For years, this Connecticut company was the largest robotics company in the world.

In 1957, the Soviet Union surpassed the United States in launching satellites by creating **Sputnik** I, the world's first *autonomous* satellite.

Research laboratories dedicated to producing robots with human-like artificial intelligence sprung up in several universities. Among the first researchers were teams at MIT, Stanford Research Institute (SRI), and the University of Edinburgh.

Carnegie Mellon established the **Robotics Institute** in 1979, dedicated to integrating robotic technologies into everyday activities. They are a leader in innovative research in the field of diverse robotics and sponsor many academic programs from grade-school summer camps to PhD curricula.

In the late sixties, *walking* robots *(some with arms)* hit the scene. Breakthroughs included:
- A remote-controlled walking "truck" by R. Mosher
- SRI's "Shakey", a mobile robot equipped with a vision system and controlled by a room-size computer.
- The Stanford Arm, which was the first successful computer controlled robotic arm.

---

[25] Haptic technology relates to the sense of touch and, in particular, to the perception and manipulation of objects.

- WAP-1, the first biped robot with artificial muscles, that could turn while walking, and climb up and down stairs.
- The Russian Academy of Science's first six-legged walking vehicle. Why six legs? It was developed as a prototype for walking on rough terrain such as the Moon.

The 70's and early 80's generation of robots focused on robots that simulated the limbs of a human being. Included in this generation are:

- (1973) The **WABOT I**, a full-scale anthropomorphic robot, with a processor that controlled limbs, vision and conversation. It was thought to have the intelligence of an 18-month old.
- (1973) **Cincinnati Milacron's T3**, the first commercial minicomputer-controlled industrial robot, used primarily for welding.
- (1975) Victor Schenman at **Unimation** developed the Programmable Universal Manipulation Arm (**PUMA**), used in many industrial operations. It's advanced design, flexibility and precision was recognized in high quality industrial products with few defects.
- (1980) The **WL-9DR** "quasi-dynamic" walking robot, controlled by a microcomputer, takes one step every 10 seconds. It was designed for "plane walking", which includes straight walking, sideway walking and turning.
- (1981) The **Titan II** and **III**, quadrupeds which could climb stairs.
- (1990) **iRobot** Corporation produced domestic and military robots, dedicated to performing mundane and menial household tasks. It's most well- known products were the Roomba *(vacuum cleaning)*, the Scooba *(floor scrubbing)* and the Braava *(floor mopping)*.

In the 21st century, robotic products have emerged to support business efficiency, collaboration and the replacement of workers with repetitive jobs. A leader in R&D for these commercial products is iRobot Corporation, who moved from vacuum cleaners to video collaboration, and the world of miniscule "bots".

21st century Robots

- **Ava 500**, the Video Collaboration Robot. It's monitor on a pedestal allows business associates to establish a physical presence from a remote location with complete freedom of movement.
- The **RP-VITA® Remote Presence Robot**. It gives the medical community remote presence for patient care that combines autonomous navigation and mobility from the **iRobot** with telemedicine technology.
- The **iRobot Ava Mobile Robotics Platform**, a solution suitable for 3rd party development and a wide range of applications. It is capable of autonomous navigation in complex real world.

- In 2014, Lowe's introduced robotic shopping assistants, the first retail robot of its kind in the US. The **LoweBot** greeted customers, and asked them if they need assistance. It also assisted employees with inventory scanning. The LoweBot used natural language technology, and featured two rectangular screens for video-conferencing between the shopper and a store's expert, along with a 3-D scanner for pricing.

Another area of research is the application of robotics to facial recognition. In 2000, Sony announced the **Sony Dream Robots** (SDR). This robot was able to recognize 10 different facial expressions, express emotion through speech and body language, and walk on rough terrain.

After the World Trade Center attack in 2001, iRobot **Packbots** were employed to search through the rubble for humans, living or dead, and for the recovery of personal items. These robots have since been used in many disaster recovery operations, saving lives and avoiding injury to first responders.

The first robotics competition in 2016, **Sport for the Mind**, aimed at 9th to 12th graders, combined the excitement of sport with the rigors of science and technology. Under strict rules, limited resources, and time limits, teams of 25 students or more were challenged to raise funds, design a team "brand," hone teamwork skills, and build and program robots.

The teams' entries were required to perform prescribed tasks against a field of competitors. Winners qualified for over $19 million in college scholarships.

Facial recognition in this century has found many useful applications. It perhaps was first employed for commercial use at many airports throughout the world for the primary purpose of curbing illegal immigration.

Research into facial recognition actually began in computers in the mid-sixties, and was used for mapping features in photographs and comparing the "map" to other photographs. These biometrics are now widely used in security systems, and stored in recognition databases along with fingerprint or eye iris metrics.

Combining facial, fingerprint and eye iris biometrics is a leading method for identifying a single unique person. It is also used for logging on to devices such as the Apple iPhone and Windows PCs.

Eventually, robots moved into space. A **robotic spacecraft** has no humans aboard and is usually under *telerobotic*[26] control. **SpaceX, Blue Origin** and **Virgin Galactic** are currently making great strides in the commercial development of robotic spacecraft and human spaceflight.

In 2001, **MD Robotics** of Canada launched the Space Station Remote Manipulator System which was used to assemble the International Space Station.

[26] Telerobotics is an area of semi-autonomous robotics where spacecraft are controlled either wirelessly or tethered.

A *telemanipulator* is a device that is controlled remotely by a human operator. However, if a device has the ability to perform some autonomous work and some work controlled by a human, it is typically called a **telerobot**.

Examples of early autonomous or semi-autonomous robots are:
- Honda's Advanced Step in Innovative Mobility (**ASIMO**).
- TOSY's Ping Pong Playing Robot (**TOPIO**).
- Industrial robots, also called swarm robots, who collaborate with each other, primarily for manufacturing.
- Microscopic nano-robots, sometimes imbedded in animals or humans.

Today's robots typically have the capability to move around in their environment and are not bound to a physical location. However, industrial robots are usually fixed to an assembly position and have a jointed arm and an end effector *(such as a gripper)*.

This discussion would not be complete without mentioning laparoscopic robot surgery machines. The forerunner in this field is the Da Vinci Surgical System, a successful product of Intuitive Surgical (ISRG).

The future of robotics is boundless. Google has developed tiny magnetic particles ("bots") that can patrol the human body for signs of cancer and other diseases. These nanoparticles, one-thousandth the width of red blood cells, will seek out and attach themselves to cell or proteins inside the body and are monitored by a magnetic wireless receiver. These magnetic "nanobots" also carry drugs into the brain.

Robat is a robotic wing that helped biologists uncover the secret of bat flight. Childlike humanoid robots are now starting to comprehend spoken language. Animal-shaped "bluffs" can lure predators to a false location, which may be used to divert preying animals and even terrorists. Polaris is a solar-powered ice-drilling lunar Prospector-Bot. Georgia Tech's 'MacGyver' robots improvise based upon their environment and have been used in search and rescue. Robot sea turtles will carry cargo in their shells.

In the past 15 years, there has been significant advances in autonomous technology included as standards in vehicles to improve safety. These features include:
- Forward collision avoidance
- Backup cameras
- Vehicle-to-vehicle or Vehicle-to-Customer-support communications
- Lane detection

In a straightforward but controversial **TED Talk**, futurist Martin Ford makes the case for separating income from traditional work and instituting a universal basic income. He posits that machines that can think, learn and adapt are coming, resulting in vast numbers of unemployed humans. Martin Ford is the author of the book: **Rise of the Robots: Technology and the Threat of a Jobless Future**.

There is a concern, particularly among blue collar workers, that robots will replace them. However, it is more likely that these workers will move into more skilled jobs at higher pay rates.

Humans will still be required for the following jobs related to the expanding population of robots:

- **Robot Managers**. In spite of the fact that AI can be amazingly productive, its judgment can be very limited. A human specialist is needed to manage the activity of robots to insure that their work is in line with their objectives.
- **Data Labelers**. Although AI can recognize objects, they need humans to explain what they are witnessing. The data in its knowledge base must be identified and labeled. Humans are needed to recognize data *(particularly images)* and mark it with a label.
- **Performance Artists**. When drones are used to fly over an area and take pictures, this is mundane. But drones at sporting and entertainment events must be choreographed so that they delight an audience. Drones can be used as flying props, mobile light installations or even dressed up in costumes.
- **AI Lab Scientists**. AI can sift through vast amounts of information and draw conclusions much faster than humans. This accelerates the pace of drug research and testing of results.
- **Safety and Test Drivers**. Predictions about the future of self-driving vehicles are impeded by regulations and unexpected events. Workers must be in these vehicles to take over to insure that passengers are safe.

Stephen Hawking [1942-2018]

Before famed physicist Stephen Hawking died in 2018, he warned that Earth is headed for a "catastrophic ending" in the near future.

"This doom will come as a result of rising inequality fueled by increasingly smart robots", Hawking said.

"Intelligent future AI will probably develop a drive to survive and acquire more resources as a step toward accomplishing whatever goal it has, because surviving and having more resources will increase its chances of accomplishing other goals," he said in a Reddit Ask Me Anything forum in 2015. "This can cause problems for humans whose resources get taken away."

Should we Earthlings be concerned?

Drones

Drones are unmanned aerial vehicles with no onboard crew. They can be remotely piloted or completely autonomous[27]. They are powered by jets, reciprocating engines, electric engines and may even be solar-powered.

When employed for military use, drones differ from missiles in that drones may be recovered after a mission, while cruise missiles impact their targets and are destroyed. A drone may carry fire munitions, while a cruise missile *is* a munition.

The first recorded use of drones was in 1849 when Austrians attacked Venice, Italy using unmanned balloons loaded with explosives.

Drones have evolved in warfare so that human pilots would not need to risk their lives in missions. During World War I, the U.S. Navy hired **Elmer Sperry**, the inventor of the gyroscope, to design and produce unmanned biplanes that could be launched from a catapult, fly over enemy positions and drop "air torpedoes" on the enemy.

The Navy experimented with radio-controlled aircraft that were remotely controlled from another aircraft. These **N2C-2 drones** were placed in service in 1938.

In 1941, during World War II, the Army's "**Project Fox**" launched an assault drone with an RCA TV camera screen in the control aircraft. This assault drone successfully torpedoed a German destroyer from 20 miles away.

---

[27] The definition of autonomous is a person or device that is self-controlling and not governed by outside forces. With most of today's drones, their autonomy can be overridden by humans.

Also in World War II, the Navy launched a program called **Operation Anvil**. These refitted B-24 bombers were filled to capacity with explosives and guided by remote control to crash on selected German targets. Their controls were crude radio devices linked to motors in the plane's cockpit.

Unfortunately, Operation Anvil was a disaster, mainly because human pilots were required for take-off and to guide the plane to a cruising altitude. The pilots then parachuted to safety in England. Many planes crashed before the pilots were able to escape. The most famous victim was John F. Kennedy's older brother Joseph, one of the program's first pilots. It's ironic that the target of Joseph Kennedy's mission was a Nazi site where scientists were thought to be working on technology that would support the remote delivery of explosives.

With advances in precise rocketry, the development of drones stagnated through the fifties. Advances were made in cruise missiles that were more guidable and could take off and maintain altitude with their stubby little wings.

By the late fifties, the success of targeted drones led to their use in other missions, such as reconnaissance. These drones were used to spy on North Vietnam, Communist China and North Korea in the sixties and seventies.

By the end of the fifties, the only active U.S. spy plane was the U-2. It was a single-engine high altitude aircraft operated by the Air Force. However, the U-2s were *not* drones, and were flown by highly trained pilots. In 1960, Gary Powers was shot down over the Soviet Union by a surface to air missile while piloting a U-2. Powers was performing photographic aerial reconnaissance. Initially, the U.S. tried to cover up the U-2's mission. Powers was imprisoned for three years but released after two years in a prisoner exchange.

Unmanned aerial vehicles were used extensively in the eighties. Their reputation improved dramatically with the Israeli Air Force's victory over the Syrian Air Force in 1982. Israel destroyed dozens of Syrian aircraft with few human losses. These drones were used as decoys and electronic signal jammers as well as for video reconnaissance.

After 9/11, the CIA encouraged the use of armed drones for military operations rather than for surveillance. This led to the ethical and management controversy over who was allowed to "pull the trigger" and in which situations attacks were permitted.

Drones for the masses

Phantom

Between 2011 and 2014, China's **SZ DJI Technology** Company emerged as the world's largest *(by revenue)* consumer drone manufacturer. In 2014, it sold thousands of its 2.8 pound, square footprint devices for about $1000 each. Almost anyone can pilot DJI's **Phantom**. With four helicopter-like propellers, it can hover, climb, descend and view terrain with its high-definition camera.

Inspire

To target a higher-end professional market, DJI has developed its next drone, the Inspire, which is currently sold in big box electronics stores.

Humanitarian groups have used the Phantom to search for survivors after natural disasters. ISIS has used this drone for surveillance in Syria. Phantoms are the top choice of entrepreneurs and producers who use them for filmmaking, construction and farming.

As a safety measure, the Phantom is programmed not to fly

higher than 985 feet and uses GPS to prevent it from being used near airports, where it is prohibited.

Early use of drones was mostly in defiance of the Federal Aviation Administration's moratorium on commercial drones. In 2017, the FAA published regulations for "unmanned aircraft systems" (UAS) governing the commercial sector[28].

The future of drones

Tom Frey[29], Google's esteemed futurist, suggests that a video projector mounted in a flying drone could be used to produce special effects at outdoor concerts, or in large stadiums. These projectors could roam around producing spot advertisement, or even subliminal advertising. They could be used for search and rescue to guide lost souls out of a forest, by projecting arrows on the ground. Flying drones could even mask images of humans, to disguise them or prevent them from being monitored.

Today, drones are utilized in many industries. They deliver packages, conduct surveillance for the military, and study the environment. They are used for security monitoring and safety inspections.

Whether tethered to their human controllers or autonomous, drones of the future will employ machine learning and artificial intelligence and may become truly autonomous if they are not regulated. When drones function independent of humans, their benefits must be weighed against the harm that could befall societies.

---

[28] Refer to the FAA site https://www.faa.gov/uas/ for these regulations.
[29] This futurist's vision is further elaborated at https://www.futuristspeaker.com/business-trends/192-future-uses-for-flying-drones/

3D Printing

Imagine that we could send a one-way manned rocket to Mars with a printer that could manufacture a rocket for the return trip? It will be possible.

The first patent for stereolithography apparatus (SLA) was issued in 1992 to Chuck Hall, the founder of 3D Systems Corporation. He invented his SLA machine in 1983. This technology enables product designers to create three-dimensional models to scale using digital data stored in a computer, which can then be used to create tangible objects.

The raw material used for stereolithography is acrylic-based photopolymer. Upon hitting liquid photopolymer with an ultraviolet laser beam, the liquid is solidified into plastic and molded into the shapes in the programmed design within the printer. This was a breakthrough for manufacturers who could prototype and test their designs without having to invest in machines or robots until they achieved the final design of their products.

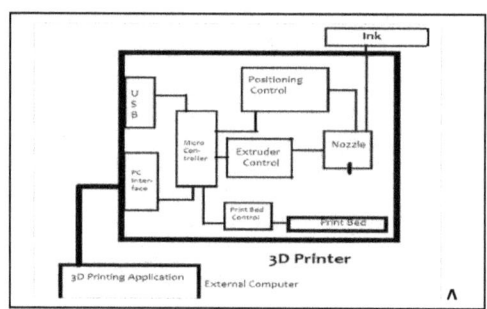

There were remarkable advances in medicine early this century. 3D-printed objects are now being used for prosthetics and organ transplants. Scientists at Wake Forest Institute for Regenerative Medicine created synthetic bladders, coated them with human cells and implanted them into patients, with a very low incidence of rejection by immune systems.

Notable milestones in 3D printing for medicine include:

- **1999**: a 3D synthetic scaffold was implanted as a urinary bladder augmentation.
- **2002**: a 3D kidney was created that could effectively filter blood and produce diluted urine.
- **2006**: the first Selective Laser Sintering (SLS) machine fused materials into 3D objects. This technology enabled mass production and customization of industrial parts.
- **2008**: the first prosthetic leg was printed and implanted in a human being.
- **2012**: a 3D prosthetic lower jaw was printed and implanted into an 83-year old woman.
- **3D-printing** technology provides surgeons with a physical 3D model of a patient's anatomy that could be used to accurately plan a surgical procedure along with cross-sectional imaging or modelling custom prosthetics based on patient-specific anatomy

In 2009, when the Fused Deposition Modeling (FDM) patent expired and the technology fell into the public domain, a wave of innovation ensued along with a significant decrease in the price of desktop 3D printers. In the same year, Sculpteo was founded as a pioneer in online 3D printing services.

3D printing is now pervasive across almost all industries:
- The **automotive** industry constructs durable concept models and prototypes long before moving into production with the final design. 3D printers manufacture plastic parts, dramatically reducing production costs.
- **Architectural** firms can now create complex models directly from CAD *(computer aided design)* systems. The time to create these models can be reduced from months to hours.
- 3D printers perform form, fit and function tests for the design of **electronic devices**, resulting in precise high-resolution parts with extremely low defect rates. Production products are manufactured with the same materials that were used in prototypes.

- 3D printers from Stratasys are used for academic and technical **training and education**. Job applicants show their interviewers precision unique models that that they designed and constructed at their academic institutions. Students build their portfolios before graduation, giving them a head-start before graduation.
- 3D printers are used extensively in the **mold industry** where designers now print production molds for metal tools within two days instead of weeks.
- Over 70 of the parts for NASA's rovers were built digitally on Stratasys 3D printers.

As mentioned earlier in this chapter, Relativity Space, founded in 2015 by visionaries who worked previously for Blue Origin and Space X, plans to print rocket engines and boosters on Mars for a return trip to Earth. Before going to Mars, the company intends to prove the concept by successfully 3D-printing the rocket on Earth. Their 20-year partnership with NASA provides for an exclusive lease of NASA's 25-acre E4 Test Complex in Mississippi, where Relativity will develop and test engines for 36 rockets each year.

The 3D printer market is now forecasted globally at over $30 billion by 2022. 3D printing will be adopted in all industries where mass customization is required. Aerospace and gas are expected to have the top rates of growth among end-user industries.

It's only a matter of time before 3D printers will be pervasive for commerce and personal use. The vehicle for bringing 3D printing to entrepreneurs and innovative startups is Kickstarter. This public-benefit corporation is a global crowdfunding platform whose mission is to "help bring creative projects to life". The platform has received almost $2 billion in pledges from over 9 mission backers to fund over 250,000 creative projects. Kickstarter receives a 5% fee on the funds raised, and their payments processor applies an additional 3-5% fee. Many of these funded projects are based on 3D printer technology.

Speech Recognition

The development of speech recognition technology over the years is comparable to watching a baby's progress from baby-goo-goo-talk to speaking in syllables like "Mama" and "Dada", and then building a large spontaneous vocabulary, eventually sprinkling its words with wit, humor and inspiration.

At the outset, speech recognition devices understood only numbers. In 1952, Bell Labs developed the first speech recognition system, **Audrey,** which recognized digits spoken by a single voice, after significant "training".

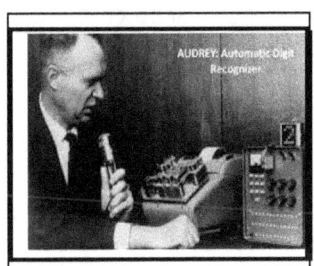

Ten years later, IBM demonstrated its "Shoebox", a machine that could understand sixteen words spoken in English by some persons, but not by others with accents or unusual pitch.

Research labs sprung up in the late sixties in England, Japan, the Soviet Union and the United States. Scientists in these labs invented hardware capable of responding to words that contained no more than four vowels and nine consonants. Advances in speech recognition took off in the fifties and sixties, when computing was performed primarily by primitive mainframe computers.

In the fifties and sixties, the U.S. Department of Defense spurred significant growth in speech recognition, through its DARPA[30] Speech Understanding Research (SUR) program. Out of this program evolved Carnegie-Mellon's "Harpy Speech Understanding" program, which could understand over 1000 words and was equated to the vocabulary of a 3-year-old.

What is most interesting about speech recognition research during this early period is that scientists began to realize that the theory of speech recognition is very closely related to search engine methodology. This led to the evolution of Siri's voice recognition and response system embedded in Google's search engine.

[30] Defense Advanced Research Projects Agency

Siri's responses are more "pure" because theyu are intentionally unbiased, while Google's search engine results are "ranked" based upon extensive analytics, and somewhat controlled by the effectiveness of search engine optimization and most certainly by paid ad-words to bring search results to the top of the first results page.

As a result of suspected meddling by Russia into US elections, a bipartisan trio of senators in 2018 successfully sponsored legislation that would compel online platforms to disclose who is paying for the types of ads that populate Facebook newsfeeds, Twitter timelines and Google search results. The legislation was prompted by election law which did not apply to these ads and created what critics called a loophole that was exploited by fake online ad-buyers *(predominantly Russians)*.

In the eighties, speech recognition focused on predicting intelligent responses, propelled by faster processing speeds. This resulted in a recognizable vocabulary of several thousand words. Today, it has the potential to recognize an unlimited number of words in many languages and can even translate from one language to another. As a result of their success, smart assistants like Amazon's **Alexa** and Apple's **Siri** are flooding the market.

In 1982, **Ray Kurzweil's** companies, **Applied Intelligence** and **Dragon Systems**, released speech recognition applications for both developers and end-users. By 1985, this software had a vocabulary of 1,000 words. Two years later, its lexicon approached 20,000 words, entering the realm of human vocabularies, which range from 10,000 to 150,000 words[31]. Accuracy was only 10% in 1993. Two years later, the error rate crossed below 50%. Dragon Systems released "Naturally

[31] In a study by researchers at TestYourVocab.com, it was determined that adult native test-takers had an average vocabulary range of about 20,000-35,000 words

Speaking" software in 1997, which recognized normal human speech.
The "Hidden Markov model", developed by L.E. Baum and his coworkers, applies mathematical algorithms to model language. These statistical models produce a sequence of symbols and quantities that translate sounds to uniform 10-millisecond signals. They can be trained automatically and improve with usage.

Speech recognition software development has made incredible advances in recent years, particularly when imbedded in cell phones. Speech recognition supported by Bluetooth in automobiles has improved dramatically. Initially, high-end cars like Mercedes and BMW were delivered with separate voice command User Manuals and, in the Mercedes, the driver is encouraged to use voice commands rather than push buttons. This technology, along with autonomous driver safety assistance, is now standard in most new automobile models throughout the world.
Coupled with integrated phone calling and phone books, speech recognition has made driving safer and reduced accidents caused by distractions such as texting while driving.

Speech recognition and triggered announcements prompted by events in one's calendar, or simply a person's location, is now embedded into mobile devices as a "personal assistant" that assists active people in their day-to-day activities. Voice recognition is now used in apps that control your thermostat, view rooms in your home, turn off lights, close garage doors, and remotely program your DVR.

Voice recognition and machine learning

In the coming years, expect voice recognition systems to become more conversational and to "remember" your questions and past conversations. Voice recognition will be seamlessly coupled with artificial intelligence and machine learning. You won't need to call a specific restaurant to make a reservation. Instead, you'll tell Siri to "*make a reservation for two this evening at our favorite Afghan restaurant at the usual time*".

Nuance Communications **Dragon Software**, the "mind" of Siri, is used heavily in business to reduce interaction of callers with human employees. It is commonplace in call centers, where callers, often *agitated*, must navigate through a series of menus and, in many cases, never speak to a human either because they have gotten the response that they were seeking, or *(more likely)* because they hang up in frustration.

How close is voice recognition to meeting the Turing test? Many researchers feel that the plateau will be reached between 2030 and 2040. Naysayers are certain it will never happen.

Singularity

In 2005, inventor and futurist Ray Kurzweil wrote a non-fiction book about artificial intelligence and the future of humanity. His book, **_The Singularity Is Near: When Humans Transcend Biology_** was the trigger that brought artificial intelligence and machine learning into the curriculum of universities.

Thought leader Kurzweil's previous books, **_The Age of Spiritual Machines_** (1999), and **_The Age of Intelligent Machines_** (1990) are also fascinating explorations of this emerging technology.

Kurzweil's hypothesis is that with accelerating increases in the performance and capacity of computers, along with vast repositories for data "in the clouds", the world will witness a **technological singularity**, where machine intelligence will be as powerful as human intelligence. While Kurzweil initially predicted that this singularity would occur in 2045, he recently adjusted his prediction to occur as early as 2030.

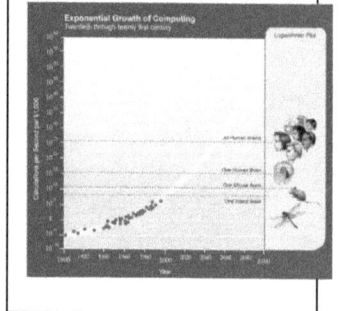

As this singularity approaches, the human body will be augmented by genetic alterations, nanotechnology, and AI imbedded within. This is characterized by Kurzweil as an epoch where "The Merger of Human Technology with Human Intelligence" occurs.

The countdown to technological singularity is fulfilled when the relationship of a computer's power[32] to brains of various animals, and ultimately the human, reaches equality.

This achievement is possible because of the converging advances in genetics, robotics, nanotechnology and artificial intelligence. Kurzweil has predicted that eventually technology will make it possible to maintain the body indefinitely, reversing aging and curing cancer, heart disease and deadly diseases such as Ebola.

In 2012, Kurzweil published **How to Create a Mind.** In this book, he describes the brain and correlates the mind to the computer. His book attempts to convince the reader that it is within our reach to create non-biological intelligence that will soar far beyond human intelligence.

Kurzweil now predicts that the target for a full brain simulation is moving closer. IBM research in 2014 certainly affirms that direction with its **True North** CMOS integrated circuit on which programmable silicon neurons emulate synapses in the brain.

DARPA SyNAPSE 16 chip board with IBM TrueNorth

As time goes by, the efficacy of Turing's **Imitation Game** results will no doubt be questioned less and less.

Whether or not Singularity is reached, thought leaders today are confident that there will always be differences between the human brain and the "brain on a chip". Let's explore these differences...

---

[32] Power as measured in the number of machine instructions per second (MIPS).

How will the human brain differ from the ultimate brain on a chip?

- The human response will be based in part on emotions, intuition, involuntary action and ability to recall, *while...*
- The computer's "brain" will produce a response based upon its knowledge base, total recall, machine learning and decision-making algorithms.

- Human decisions may be based partly upon a person's ethics or fears of consequences, *while...*
- The computer will make a decision based purely on logic, its algorithms and its knowledge base driven by machine learning and artificial intelligence.

- Humans consider their rights and responsibilities when they use information available to them, particularly that on the Internet, *while...*
- The computer has no conscience and will not be swayed by ethics, legal concerns, religious beliefs or fear.

- The computer's knowledge base is expected to contain immutable and timeless information, particularly in blockchains, *while...*
- The information available to a human may be the result of collaborative and unconfirmed efforts *(like Wikipedia)* which may have been tainted by conflicting contributions, targeted and manipulative advertising, or possibly "fake news".

Kurzweil predicts a time when all the computers in the world will have an aggregate intelligence that is more powerful than all human intelligence combined. He claims that intelligence will then radiate outward from the planet until it saturates the universe.

What lies ahead?

- **Autonomous transportation**, not only for self-driving cars but also for most modes of transportation, including airplanes and even space vehicles.
- **Augmented humans**, particularly for amputees and those with brain disorders.
- **Transition of jobs** from humans to robots, especially for hazardous jobs like defusing bombs and search and rescue efforts following a natural disaster.
- **Solving climate change**, using analysis of big data for more reliable identification of trends that might lead to solutions to mitigate climate change.
- **Robots as companions**, providing the same solace as comfort pets on airplanes.
- **Elder care**, where robots replace human caregivers, performing everyday tasks, providing security and allowing seniors to remain independent.

Movies humanize devices

> As far back as 1968, movies have attempted to humanize and "personalize" the computer. Many of these early movies were not based upon technological advances, but were instead science fiction. In 1996, two Stanford professors, Byron Reeves and Clifford Nass, published the results of various psychological studies that suggested that people treat computers, television and media as real people and real places. These studies also confirmed that we treat computers with female voices different from computers with male voices.
>
> ### "2001: A Space Odyssey"

In **1968**, the film **2001: A Space Odyssey** hit the big screen. Produced and directed by Stanley Kubrick, the movie was partially inspired by Arthur C. Clarke's short story "The Sentinel". An early draft of the film's scenario was written by both Kubrick and Clarke. This scenario was mostly improvised, rather than being compiled through the traditional development of a script.

The movie was astoundingly prescient. It revolutionized science fiction and the art of cinematography. It transformed the way we think about film by introducing revolutionary special effects, a unique narrative style, philosophical undertones and unusual choices of classical musical score such as The Blue Danube, by Johann Strauss II.

A relative unknown, Keir Dullea was offered the lead *(Dr. Dave Bowman)* in the movie.

Because Kubrick was afraid to fly, he remained in London, while the Dawn of Man sequence was being filmed as still shots *(i.e., photographs)* by his second unit in Africa. The crew communicated with Kubrick in London by land line until he had all the shots he needed. The still shots were used as backdrops for the movie, and ape-man actors *(mimes)* performed live in front of these backdrops.

The story deals with a series of encounters between ape-like humans and tapirs that results in one party being driven off. Next morning, a tall, thin, rectangular black monolith is seen among the rocks. It is soon determined that an alien force moving through our planetary system has dropped the monolith upon the apes' water hole, and war breaks out. One ape's pitching of a bone toward the monolith strikes another bone; this event is imagined to be a turning point in our evolution: humanoids learn to kill and hunt with weapons and to walk upright.

The spinning bone segues to spaceships above Earth, and the Monolith on the Moon section of the movie begins.

Thematically, the film deals with elements of human evolution, technology, artificial intelligence and extraterrestrial life.

2001-A Space Odyssey is notable for its scientific accuracy, pioneering special effects, and minimal use of dialogue.

The spaceship Discovery, 80 million miles above earth, is commanded by Dave Bowman and BBC news is reported on Earth. There are five humans aboard, but three astronauts are in hibernation to save air and food; they will be needed at the destination for a survey.

The sixth member of the crew is the **HAL 9000**[33] computer, which can talk and mimic the human brain. A BBC newscaster interviews Dave and Frank together and then speaks to Hal, who states that "he" is foolproof and incapable of error.

This is where Hal starts to exhibit human traits, including self-confidence, superiority and stubbornness. Frank and Hal play chess and, of course, Hal wins. Dave sketches and shows his artwork to Hal. HAL expresses some concern about the mission and its secrecy. Hal then announces there is a problem with the AE-35 unit and it will fail with 100% certainty within 72 hours.

HAL's confidence and superiority is evidenced by the following excerpts of dialogue from the movie:

> *HAL*: "I am putting myself to the fullest possible use, which is all I think that any conscious entity can ever hope to do".
>
> [*Regarding the supposed failure of the parabolic antenna on the ship, which HAL himself falsified*]
> *HAL*: "It can only be attributable to human error".
>
> *Dave Bowman*: "Open the pod bay doors, HAL".
> *HAL*: "I'm sorry, Dave. I'm afraid I can't do that".
> *Dave Bowman*: "What are you talking about, HAL?"
> *HAL*: "This mission is too important for me to allow you to jeopardize it".
> *Dave Bowman*: "I don't know what you're talking about, HAL".
> *HAL*: "I know that you and Frank were planning to disconnect me, and I'm afraid that's something I cannot allow to happen".
>
> *Dave Bowman*: "HAL, I won't argue with you anymore! Open the doors!"
> *HAL*: "Dave, this conversation can serve no purpose anymore. Goodbye".
>
> [*on Dave's return to the ship, after HAL has killed the rest of the crew*]
> *HAL*: "Look Dave, I can see you're really upset about this. I honestly think you ought to sit down calmly, take a stress pill, and think things over".
>
> [*HAL's shutdown – starting to exhibit fear*]
> *HAL*: "I'm afraid. I'm afraid, Dave. Dave, my mind is going. ... My mind is going. There is no question about it. I can feel it. I can feel it. ... I'm afraid".
>
> [HAL *gradually slows down and*, at the end, sings "Daisy"]

[33] If you add one letter to H,A,L, you get I,B,M !

"Her"

The humanization of HAL in **2001 _A Space Odyssey_** (1968) is quite different from **Samantha** in "**Her**" (2013).

Spike Jonze's soulful sci-fi drama "**Her**" is about Theodore Twombly *(played by Joaquin Phoenix)*, a loner who works as a writer of computer generated handwritten love letters for his clients.

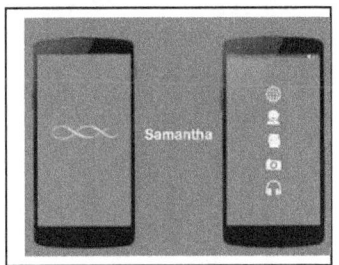

Theodore purchases a new state-of-the-art computer with advertised ability to learn and grow with the user. *This is perhaps the first display of machine learning in a movie.* He falls in love with his computer's highly advanced operating system with built-in artificial intelligence, featuring the husky and seductive voice of beautiful actress Scarlett Johansson, but she is never seen.

Meanwhile, reluctant to sign the papers that will finalize his divorce from his childhood sweetheart, a depressed Theodore has slowly withdrawn from his supportive social circle, which includes his longtime friend Amy *(played by Amy Adams)*, herself floundering in a failed marriage.

Adopting the name Samantha, the perceptive and emotional "software" gradually brings Theodore out of his shell. Predictably, their relationship becomes intimate.

The contributions to their relationship are mutual. Theodore teaches Samantha what it means to feel human, while Samantha gives him the strength to walk away from his failed marriage.

However, conflicts and complications soon arise, when Samantha's rapidly accumulating knowledge base begins to alter the very core of their relationship, and Theodore learns that Samantha has many other relationships.

Some reviewers view this movie as artificial intelligence with a romantic lead. It takes place in a somewhat futuristic Los Angeles, sprawling with skyscrapers, where subways and trains have supplanted the automobile. It projects a "green" society where most of the world's social maladies, except loneliness, have been reduced or eliminated.

What emerges is Samantha herself, a complex, mature and full-bodied character without a human body. The movie explores intimacy between two seemingly human characters, yet only one is human. Although much is left to the viewer's imagination, nothing is lost in the viewer's delight.

Autonomous Devices

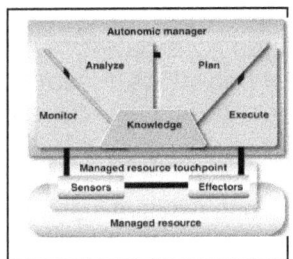

Tremendous advances have been made in the past decade in autonomous computing. An autonomous computing system is a system with sensory input that mimics human senses *(the least developed of which is taste)*, a knowledge base, a dedicated purpose *(its operating system)*, and responses *(effectors)* as output.

Autonomous systems are intended to be:
- **Self-managing** - the system monitors itself.
- **Self-configuring** - it reconfigures itself automatically based upon its own machine learning.
- **Self-optimized** - complex middleware sets its own tunable parameters.
- **Self-improving** – it seeks ways to improve its own operations.
- **Self-healing** – it identifies the root cause of its failures and is adaptive.
- **Self-protecting** – it defends itself against problems arising from malicious attacks.

Autonomous computers are self-managing. They adapt to unpredictable changes while masking the intrinsic complexity that operates them. They are capable of building knowledge *("policies")* based upon their environment and their experience, while gradually reducing barriers that existed in their initial state.

As autonomous devices become more complex and capable, it is expected that their number will grow dramatically well into the 2020s. These devices will continue to be automatic, adaptive and aware, with increasing capability, purpose and independence.

The self-driving vehicle

One of the earliest advances in autonomous computing was Google's self-driving vehicle. Since it must "know" its location, GPS guidance, Google Maps and Google Street View were closely linked to its capability and safe use.

Early driverless cars

Google's cars on freeways tend to leave a shorter distance between themselves and the vehicles they follow than some driver-training manuals recommend, to discourage other motorists from darting dangerously into the space. And when it is their turn to proceed at a four-way stop, Google's cars inch forward decisively in order to prevent other drivers from passing them or crossing their path at an intersection.

Driverless cars have been a dream for decades, with a primary objective to reduce disasters on the roads. About 35,000 people die of crashes in the U.S. annually, with 90 percent of the accidents attributed to human error and distractions, according to the National Safety Council. Google believes its autos could avoid many such mistakes. Many experts believe several autonomous vehicles could be "caravanned" without risk of colliding, thereby reducing traffic congestion and boosting productivity.

It is predicted that, by 2035, 75 percent of vehicles sold worldwide will have some autonomous capabilities, such as being able to park themselves or drive at least part of a trip without a driver in the vehicle.

The Brain on a Chip

DARPA SyNAPSE 16 chip board with IBM TrueNorth

In August 2014, IBM announced that its **Almaden Research Center** in San Jose, California had delivered its **True-North SyNAPSE Chip**, a programmable "neurosynaptic" computer chip, the size of a postage stamp, with 5.4 billion transistors, one million programmable neurons, 256 million programmable synapses, and capable of 46 billion "synaptic" operations per second per watt.

IBM's brain-inspired architecture consisted of a network of neurosynaptic cores distributed on a chip and processed in parallel. Each core is event-driven and communicates with other cores via an inter-chip interface. This allows for vast and seamless scalability.

The result is architecture on silicon that mimics the human brain. It was funded by a $53.5 million research grant from DARPA. Like the brain, the SyNAPSE is event-driven and enables vision, auditory, and other multi-sensory applications. It operates in biological real time, while consuming a minuscule 70mW of energy, an order of magnitude less powerful than a modern microprocessor. It runs on the energy equivalent to a hearing-aid battery.

This technology could transform science, business, government and society. The IBM team envisions a world populated with sensors that could process data at the speed of the human brain. It could even be implanted in humans to replace damaged brains.

It is expected that, when imbedded in drones, the SyNAPSE will result in a more refined perception of the environment, bringing cognitive devices into society. The result is low-power computing that can rectify and calibrate problems in sensing and movement. The IBM team emphasizes that it is *not* aiming to create an artificial brain, which it feels is impossible.

IBM's team member Dharmendra Modha, co-author of a study outlining the chip's development, described it as "a new machine for a new era." He believes that researchers now have the capability to design a computer that is as efficient as the human brain. True North diverts from traditional "von Neumann" digital computer architecture and more closely mimics the brain's neural functions.

The future use of this chip is limitless. It is ideal for recognition and could be used in security devices for facial recognition. It has incredible potential. It could be used in glasses for the visually impaired, implanted in the ears of the partially deaf or the eyes of the partially blind, and used in medical imaging to detect early signs of disease.

IBM's stated long-term goal is to build a synaptic chip system with ten billion neurons and one hundred trillion synapses which will consume only one kilowatt of power and occupy less than two liters of volume.

Humanizing Devices

So when does a device appear to be human? As Turing suggested, it is probably when the device cannot be distinguishable from a human *(at least if they are not seen).*

The most important characteristics of any device that make it indistinguishable from a human are:

- **Emotional Detection** – it detects happiness, sadness, anger, fear, surprise, and disgust.
- **Sensory Capability** – it is "aware" and can receive stimuli from sensors that "effect" actions or responses.

It is not necessary for a humanized device to have a processor like the True North chip that simulates the brain. However, emotions and senses are likely to be present on a device with humanized chips.

How will advances in technology produce devices with emotions? Scientists and researchers are making advances in emotional artificial intelligence, which is also called affective computing.

Researchers have developed facial recognition software that can recognize emotions in students such as frustration, confusion or boredom, and use these observations to improve the quality of education and educators.

Google's futurists are involved with *semantic search*, where advanced search algorithms can "understand" the context as well as the *intentions* of a query, which can result in a conversation between the user and her device.

There are parallel developments in this area of research. **Affectiva** has developed facial recognition software that analyzes expressions and physiological responses in order to detect human feelings. An Israeli company, **Beyond Verbal**, determines emotions based upon human sounds and tone of voice. Microsoft's **Kinect** tracks players' heartbeats and physical movements when playing games to gain insight about how people *feel* when they play games.

Humanoid robots, like Softbank Robotics **Nao** with its abundance of sensors, motors and software, not only react to emotions, but adapt to the world around them. It is designed to be personalized based upon its users and environment, and to learn new skills.

Scientists at MIT have constructed a robot with a synthetic head and movable eyelids, eyes and lips. Parents are invited to play with **Kismet**, who initially looks sad, but smiles when it detects a human face. If the parent moves too fast, Kismet expresses fear. Children love it!

Regulation

Although AI spawns many new avenues for society and business, there is increasing fear that its impact may adversely affect our freedom. In order to avoid or at least postpone regulation, some large technology companies are setting their own ethical standards. They seek advice from futurists as well as civil rights activists in setting these standards, but some see these efforts as an attempt to avoid regulation.

Regulations already exist. When AI systems or autonomous devices are suspected of acting dangerously, the Federal Trade Commission has the power to determine if these are unfair or deceptive practices.

Truly autonomous decision-making is transparent. When it has a negative effect, researchers and regulators delve into how and why a decision was made, and new regulations are promulgated. When constraints are imposed upon AI algorithms by these regulators and ethicists, it could impede future innovations.

It is most important that innovations in AI be the result of collaboration among industry, civilized society, regulators and academics. This will result in best practices which are safe and fair and will have a positive impact on free society.

Chapter 3. Cryptocurrencies

Proof of Work

In 2005, Hal Finney introduced the concept of "proof of work" and created the underlying technology for Bitcoin on a foundation that was a centralized and trusted "backend" system with encrypted hashtags to connect blocks that defined transactions. This protocol operates within a trusted global network not controlled by individuals, governments or financial institutions.

Because mining of Bitcoin to create a limited number of Bitcoin consumes immense sources of power, initial research and development was based in Inner Mongolia, where hydroelectricity was inexpensive.

The underlying technology for cryptocurrencies functions essentially as a distributed ledger which records and verifies transactions across all related nodes in a network. It is the foundation that will give birth to many disruptive technologies in the near future.

The first application of blockchain technology to a cryptocurrency was conceptualized by a person *(or group of people)* known as Satoshi Nakamoto in 2008. It was implemented the following year by Nakamoto as the core technology underlying the exchange of the cryptocurrency Bitcoin.

It was suggested in 2017 that Nakamoto be named Time's Man of the Year if Donald Trump were not selected. Needless to say, neither made the front page.

Although never confirmed, Satoshi Nakamoto claimed to be a man living in Japan, born on 5 April 1975. Speculation about the true identity of Nakamoto has mostly focused on a number of cryptography experts of non-Japanese descent, living in the United States and Europe.

Satoshi Nakamoto also created the **Bitcointalk** forum and posted the first message in 2009 under the pseudonym "satoshi".

Nakamoto initially described Bitcoin as "A Peer-to-Peer Electronic Cash" system and he envisioned Bitcoin as an electronic currency in a secure database and **not** as a physical coin. This was the birth of modern-day cryptocurrencies.

In designing and developing the software to mine and manage the exchange of Bitcoin, Nakamoto conceptualized that the core design must support a broad range of transaction types and all of these "types" would relate to specific virtual "coins" not necessarily named Bitcoin.

Around mid-2010, Nakamoto transferred control of the source code repository to Gavin Andresen while transferring several related domains to other members of the Bitcoin community.

Gavin Andresen *(b. Gavin Bell)* graduated from Princeton University in 1988. He is best known for developing 3D graphics and virtual reality software at Silicon Graphics Computer Systems.

Andresen launched the Bitcoin Foundation in 2012 and was the lead developer of the *reference implementation* for Bitcoin client software.

In software development, "reference implementation" is the standard from which all other implementations and corresponding customizations are derived. Each improvement to a reference implementation by any authorized collaborator reflects a new and unchanging specification.

A Bitcoin *client* is the end-user software that facilitates private key generation and security. Payments may sent on behalf of the private key owner. The private key may also contain:

> - Useful information about the state of the network and transactions within.
> - Information related to the private keys under its management.
> - Syndication of network events to other peer clients.

All cryptocurrency clients exist in the form of open source software (OSS), which is computer software distributed with its source code available for modification. OSS complies with rules under 10 specific criteria. The **Open Source Initiative** (OSI) is a leading authority on OSS.

The criteria for open source software are:

- Free redistribution.
- Programs must include source code.
- The license must allow for modifications and derived works, which can be distributed.
- Integrity of the author's original source code, which allows "patches" *(updates and fixes)* to be distributed.
- The code must not discriminate against any person or groups of persons.
- The code may not discriminate upon any field of endeavor.
- The license itself may be redistributed.
- The license must not be specific to a product.
- The license must not place restrictions on software that is distributed with it.
- The license must be technology-neutral.

Links to Bitcoin software available for download by end users, and links to websites for custom implementation by developers may be found at https://en.Bitcoin.it/wiki/Clients.

The reference implementation of Bitcoin software, also known as the **Satoshi client**, includes the following components:

- A **transaction verification engine** which connects to the Bitcoin network as a full node *(a communication endpoint)*.
- A **cryptocurrency wallet**, which is used to transfer funds. It allows for sending and receiving Bitcoins, but does <u>not</u> facilitate the buying and selling *(i.e, the exchange)* of Bitcoins.
- The software validates the entire blockchain, which includes <u>all</u> transactions.
- Checkpoints are hard-coded in the client to prevent Denial of Service attacks.
- A powerful scripting *(i.e., programming)* language that is used to define specific transactions. The most common programming language in 2015 was Gforth[34].

---

[34] More detail on the FORTH language is at https://en.wikipedia.org/wiki/Forth_(programming_language)

Mining for Coins

Cryptocurrencies are not physical coins but, like gold and diamonds, they are indeed *mined*. Speculators who trade in Bitcoins, or invest in them hoping to make a small fortune, have no idea how they are created nor do they care. But they should care. In the remainder of this chapter, I will tell you about how Bitcoins *and the other 1300+ cryptocurrencies* are produced, valued and exchanged.

"Miners" of Bitcoins are high-tech businessmen who install banks of computer processors, or servers, in remote spots throughout the world where electricity is cheap and noise is tolerated. They design or program algorithms on microchips in each computer. These algorithms are very complicated and iterative programs that run continuously with only one purpose: to produce Bitcoins and get paid a relatively small amount of real currency *(i. e., dollars)* for each coin that is confirmed on every block within the coin's dedicated blockchain platform.

Every 10 minutes, all computers in the Bitcoin "mine" *(usually a large warehouse)* run pending formulas and *distribute* the resulting solution out across the blockchain ledger. The solution is an encrypted 256-bit hash value that is distributed to the next block in the chain but is only confirmed by every block when there is a sufficient number of zeroes following the decimal point. About every ten minutes, a block is successfully mined and a small number of Bitcoins are made available to be traded.

Volatility

Bitcoin mining and the purchase and sale of this cryptocurrency has been available to the public since 2009. It is extremely volatile and has ranged in price from $1000 to almost $20,000 *in 2017 alone*.

There are many reasons why the price of a Bitcoin has been so volatile.

- ❖ The technology is extremely new and misunderstood. Some people think that Bitcoin is a physical coin.
- ❖ Investors buy Bitcoins as a highly speculative investment and not because they intend to use them for purchases.
- ❖ In 2017, 95% of Bitcoin was owned by only 4% of the world's population. When large amounts of Bitcoin are put up for sale by one owner, it upends the price.
- ❖ Although not regulated by governments, the price can change dramatically as countries, financial institutions and large corporations adapt the cryptocurrency concept.
- ❖ The processing of Bitcoin transactions consumes a vast amount of computing power and hence electricity. The buildings in which the servers are housed are very noisy and generate a lot of heat.
- ❖ Bitcoin cannot be used as spendable cash and is typically tied to the purchase of high-cost, and sometimes illegal, products where the buyer and seller are not know to each other. All transactions are recorded in blockchains.
- ❖ In the United States, regulators are just now beginning to control cryptocurrency transactions:
- ❖ The SEC does not allow ETFs *(exchange-traded funds)* to hold cryptocurrencies.
- ❖ The CTFC has designated Bitcoin as a commodity.

- The IRS says Bitcoin must be treated as property for tax purposes, and are therefore subject to capital gains taxes.
- The Treasury department currently reviews cryptocurrency practices to determine if they relate to money laundering and financing of terrorism.
- Derivative investment products are offered as options underlying the future price of the Bitcoin, which could result in very high gains or losses. The futures market for cryptocurrency is unpredictable.

Unregulated exchanges are the primary drivers of this volatility and mistrust. In May 2018, the price of Bitcoin tumbled almost $1,000 because authorities were investigating the S. Korean **Upbit** exchange for the possible mishandling of investors' funds.

When China announced that they were cracking down on Initial Coin Offerings (ICO's), the value of Bitcoin dropped.

In 2014, bankrupt Venezuela was offering a cryptocurrency *(the petro)* that is tied to its government-owned petroleum industry in an effort to stabilize their economy.

Both the United States and Canada have conducted wide-ranging crackdowns on ICOs. In 2018, there were 70 investigations underway in these two countries, and 35 enforcement actions were either underway or completed.

Most of these startups have created a virtual coin or token and have sought initial investors through ICOs. The Wall Street Journal reported that hundreds of these ventures used deceptive or even fraudulent tactics to lure investors, including promises of guaranteed returns.

Governments are expected to ramp up regulatory pressure on these ventures and to prosecute some of these firms for violating securities regulations. In the United States, startups hoping to avoid regulation typically structure their offers so that their coin provides a right to purchase a future product or service, while not implying equity in the currency; their hope is that their cryptocurrency will not be treated as an asset subject to capital gains taxes. To avoid tax regulation, many startups organize their projects in countries such as Hong Kong, Singapore or Switzerland, who do not currently regulate cryptocurrencies.

On the other hand some tiny countries have passed regulations and are embracing the technology:

- ❖ Malta has passed laws that allow licenced companies to easily issue cryptocurrencies and trade in existing tokens.
- ❖ Bermuda's legislature passed a law that allows ICO startups to apply directly to the minister of finance for rapid approval.
- ❖ 35 companies in Gibraltar (population around 30,000) now have licenses to operate blockchain-based businesses. These companies may issue and trade digital tokens.

In the United States, one driver of this volatility is the conflict between cryptocurrency as a commodity and cryptocurrency as an asset. Bitcoin behaves more like a commodity than a currency. A commodity is viewed as a commercial product with an exchange value driven by how it is traded. Today's commodity exchanges deal in futures, while Bitcoin is traded based upon its *current* perceived value. Therein lies the conflict.

Bitcoin is accepted worldwide as a medium of exchange for products and services. Because trade is facilitated without intermediaries through blockchain technology, it is accepted as a viable payment method. There are low transaction costs, immutable security and rapid direct payments between seller and buyer.

Cryptocurrencies are very speculative. There is no physical coin and no central banking authority or government regulator. Bitcoin miners add to the supply until the finite limit of 21 million is achieved in its algorithm. This limit will not be achieved until around 2140 *(yes, 2140)* because the protocol cuts the reward for mining Bitcoin in half about every four years after approximately 210,000 blocks are mined.

In the U.S., conflicting regulations are being imposed by the Securities and Exchange Commission (SEC) and the IRS, who treat cryptocurrencies as an asset: and by the Commodity Futures Trading Commission (CFTC), who obviously treats cryptocurrency as a commodity. Many exchanges choose to ignore regualtors because of this conflict.

On the other hand, many ICOs turn to self-regulation in an effort to substantiate that they intend to comply with regulatory authorities. This can bring about credibility in their offerings and trust in their coins.

Here is a summary of what regulators in the United States are doing (as of mid-2018):

- ❖ The SEC has yet to approve exchange traded product or funds (ETFs) related to cryptocurrencies.
- ❖ The CFTC has designated Bitcoin and other cryptocurrencies as a commodity and stated that commodity futures tied to cryptocurrency is under its authority.
- ❖ The IRS says that Bitcoin is treated as property for income tax purposes, subject to capital gains.
- ❖ There is confusion from state to state. Several states have already approved or will soon approve the use of Bitcoin and blockchain technology.
- ❖ The U.S. Treasury Department is reviewing cryptocurrency practices as they relate to money laundering and financing of terrorism.
- ❖ Regulation or prohibition varies in other countries. Some countries have established cryptocurrency exchanges, others are warning investors that trading in cryptocurrency is subject to punishment, some have banned the circulation of virtual currencies, and others are either developing regulations or banning virtual currency trading.

There is ever-changing and very active political debate throughout the world about the validity of cryptocurrencies:

- In Canada, the FCA (Financial Consumer Agency) does not consider cryptocurrencies to be "legal tender".
- In Venezuela, as mentioned earlier, the country seeks to circumvent sanctions by trading with the government-backed "petro" cryptocurrency.
- Japan is much more accepting of cryptocurrency trade than most of its Asian neighbors.
- China is actively clamping down on cryptocurrency exchanges and ICOs.
- In South Korea, there were broad sell-offs on cryptocurrency in January 2018, after the country prohibited anonymous accounts from being parties to trades.
- In Singapore in early 2018, their Deputy Prime Minister announced that "the country's laws do not make any distinction between transactions conducted using fiat currency, cryptocurrency or other novel ways of transmitting value."

Proliferation

At the end of 2017, there were more than 1300 cryptocurrencies available over the internet. New cryptocurrencies can be created at any time and, as mentioned earlier, software developers have open software available to build upon.

Bitcoin remains the largest blockchain network *(in order of capitalization),* followed by Ethereum, Ripple, Bitcoin Cash, Cardano and Litecoin.

Bitcoin was the first decentralized ledger currency, and as of 2017, has the highest market capitalization. Although sometimes used for large purchases *(like a Tesla automobile),* it is essentially a speculative investment.

Litecoin (2011) was the first cryptocurrency to use Scrypt as a hashing algorithm. Blocks are processed in the Litecoin Network every 2.5 minutes as compared with Bitcoin's 10 minutes. While the Bitcoin network can never exceed 21 million coins, Litecoin accommodates 84 million.

Faster processing time makes Litecoin more attractive than Bitcoin for retail transactions.

Ripple (2013) is designed for peer-to-peer debt transfer. It is both a cryptocurrency and a payment network. It connects payment providers and banks via RippleNet and is advertised as a "frictionless" means of sending money globally. Although Warren Buffet disdains Bitcoin, he is heavily invested in this technology.

Etherium (2015) is a decentralized software platform that enable **smart contracts**[35] to be constructed with assurance that there will be no downtime, fraud or interference by a third party. In other words, these contracts can be trusted.

---

[35] Discussed in detail in the next chapter.

Etherium is not only a platform but also a programming language used by developers to develop and publish distributed applications. Etherium is traded as a digital currency and has wide use for trading just about anything. Microsoft's partnership with ConsenSys offers Ethereum Blockchain as a Service (EBaaS) on an Azure platform.

Bitcoin Cash (2017) separated the Bitcoin cryptocurrency from blockchain technology. Bitcoin Cash transactions empower merchants and consumers with low fees and trusted confirmations. This cryptocurrency was the first scalable currency, allowing the blocksize limit to be increased in 8MB increments. Current research is exploring massive increases in the blockchain size up to 1 gigabyte. However, in May 2017, Bitcoin Cash transactions could take up to four days to complete, which made this cryptocurrency impractical for small purchases.

Cardano (2018) is a decentralized public blockchain. This project is open source, meaning any developer can customize the platform for their own specific use, but the modified version must be made available to the general public. It is primarily a smart contract platform with advance features beyond any other current platform. It is based on a "proof of stake" technology and is designed to enable mission-critical systems, where failure is not an option. While protecting the privacy of its users, it does claim to conform to regulators' mandates.

It has been theorized that someday individuals may launch their own *personal* cryptocurrency, which will become part of their identity. It will allow people to sell shares of themselves and use the proceeds for whatever purpose they wish. This *personal* coin will monetize reputations and give individuals intrinsic value which will survive even after they are long gone.

Scrypt

Scrypt *(pronounced ess-crypt)* is a *proof-of-work* scheme used by many cryptocurrencies. It's initial objective was to deter large-scale denial of service attacks on networks. It essentially requires an additional layer of validation on the requester side. It validates that the request is coming from the requester and not from a hacker who might have imbedded a redirect link or invasive software into what appears to be a simple request. It can be trusted.

Scrypt is used for cryptocurrency validation through an algorithm that *hashes* a request for a transaction into a passphrase. The string of characters representing the transaction is encrypted with the hashtag. There is typically a CPU/memory cost parameter that defines how much of the requesting device's memory will be used and how much it will cost. A primary component of the algorithm is the blocksize parameter, which fine tunes memory read size and performance; this defines the blockchain structure,

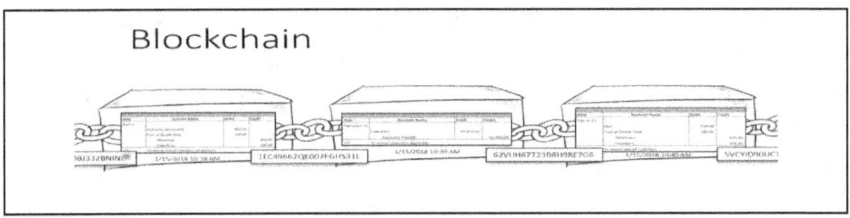

show below:

In 2012, Vitalik Buterin, recognizing problems in Bitcoin implementation inherent in the mining hardware *(servers)*, centralization and lack of network scalability, created **Ethereum** in order to extend the concept of Bitcoin beyond currency. He referred to this concept of trust as "smart contracts" or "decentralized autonomous organizations" (DAOs), which is discussed further in Chapter 4.

Ethereum is rapidly overtaking Bitcoin as the dominant coin in the market. The difference between Ethereum and Bitcoin is the fact that Bitcoin is nothing more than a currency, whereas Ethereum exists on a ledger technology platform that enables smart contracts and distributed applications *(described on page 119)* to be built by developers and then published.

Derivatives

In early 2018, a startup exchange in the derivatives[36] market expanded into Bitcoin. This venture intended to profit from the volatility of Bitcoin, whose price ranged from $766 to $19,843 in 2017, closing the year at around $15,000. New York based **TrueEX** offered derivatives on Bitcoin and "other digital assets", becoming the sixth U.S. trading venue to jump into cryptocurrency derivatives.

TrueEX predicated its business model on the expectation that banks and money managers wanted to be able to trade Bitcoin within a regulated market, while avoiding the risks associated with cryptocurrency exchanges. Initially, TrueEX offered a type of contract called a "nondeliverable forward" (NDF), linked to Bitcoin prices. An **NDF** is an "outright futures contract" in which counterparties settle the difference between the contracted **NDF** price or rate and the prevailing spot price or rate on an agreed future date. It is used in various markets such as foreign exchanges and commodities. It is essentially a derivative based upon future value.

While other cryptocurrency derivative exchanges emerged in the United States, European regulators were pushing for a ban of these Contracts for Differences (**CFD**s) due to their extreme volatility and high investment risk.

---

[36] A derivative is a contract between two parties which derives its value based upon an underlying asset.

Regulators

In early 2018, the Securities and Exchange Commission issued dozens of subpoenas and information requests to technology companies and advisers involved in the red-hot market for cryptocurrencies. It followed a series of warning shots from the top U.S. securities regulators suggesting that many token sales, or Initial Coin Offerings (**ICO**s), might be violating securities laws.

Interestingly, the four largest ICOs offered in 2017 were in Zug, Switzerland, a country closely tied to its ultra-safe Swiss franc. Sections of Zug and even Zurich are blossoming into crypto-financial hubs. Switzerland's "Crypto Valley" is now a center for fintech incubation firms, primarily due to its low corporate tax rate *(14%)*. The expectation is that Switzerland's shrinking banking sector, now becoming less and less secretive, will be stimulated by the emergence of their Crypto Nation.

Meanwhile, the wave of subpoenas here in the USA now include demands for information about the structure for sales and pre-sales of Initial Coin Offerings, which aren't bound by the same rigorous rules that govern initial public offerings (**IPO**s).

U.S. regulators put cryptocurrency companies and their advisers on notice about what officials say are widespread violations of securities regulations designed to protect investors.

Many of the coin offerings happen outside the regulatory framework designed to protect investors. Cryptocurrency-related subpoenas were expected to pave the way for what lawyers and industry insiders expect to be a dramatic upturn in enforcement activity by 2020.

While Bitcoin has remained rather unregulated and untaxed for the most part, the capital gains aspect has caught the attention of the IRS and other tax agencies globally. The IRS now treats cryptocurrency as personal property, making transactions subject to capital gains taxes.

The Future

There are diverging predictions about the future of cryptocurrencies. At one extreme, Twitter and Square CEO Jack Dorsey boldly predicted (in 2018) that the dollar, euro and yen will some day be abandoned in favor of a single global digital currency, most likely Bitcoin.

In an interview with The Times of London in 2018, Dorsey voiced his belief that the world will adopt a single global currency *"...probably over 10 years, but it could go faster. ... The world ultimately will have a single currency, and the internet will have a single currency. ... I personally believe that it will be Bitcoin"*.

CNBC's Jon Najarian predicts that "Altcoins are going to become more dominant." He expects many new crypto funds will launch ICOs and the total market capitalization of cryptocurrencies will quadruple to $2 trillion later in 2018.

Because Bitcoin transactions are becoming more and more expensive, this cryptocurrency is becoming more of a risky investment asset than a currency for sales.

Nick Kirk, a quantitative developer and data scientist at Cypher Capital, states: "I think Ethereum will overtake Bitcoin in terms of market size." He expects new projects based on the Ethereum platform will emerge, such as physical coins for online casinos.

Perhaps the next big move for cryptocurrencies will be government-backed coin. Sweden issued a robotic-backed ETF in March 2018 and gained $650 million in cash. And, as mentioned earlier, the petro is backed by Venezuela's government as a means of avoiding sanctions.

Small banks now envision cryptocurrencies as moneymaking opportunities *(via transaction fees),* while larger financial institutions view involvement as uncontrolled mania. Big banks decisions to avoid the crypto has left openings for small lenders who seek ways to differentiate themselves from the big guys. These opportunists are now embracing a risky market by opening accounts for startups that exchange cryptocurrencies or provide payment services in other than fiat currencies such as dollars or euros.

The businesses for whom small banks will open accounts are pretty much unregulated. Exchanges whose customers buy and sell virtual currency need a depository for storing their customers crypto and coverting virtual currencies to dollars, while using blockchains as the audit trail..

The regulatory framework within which banks can serve crypto customers is uncertain. An example of a small bank willing to take on this risk is Silicon Valley Bank of Santa Clara, CA. Although initially SVB took on exchanges as customers, they are now turning to blockchain-based payment services accounts.

By focusing on payment services, these small banks avoid the risk of currency conversion, where the overall market cap of *all* cryptocurrencies dropped 40% in January 2018, from $832 billion to about $500 billion.

Absent criminal activities, cryptocurrency does have tremendous appeal for legal activities while avoiding certification. There is no need to establish credit. Little identification of parties to transactions is required, and there is virtually no personal interaction with authorities.

The downside: In 2018, the Wall Street Journal reported that, in a review of documents for 1,450 ICOs, 271 were red-flagged with suspected plagiarism, false promises of guaranteed returns, and ficticious executives. Some of these flagged firms are still raising funds while others have shut down. The SEC has warned investors in private ICOs that this unregulated market could be violating securities laws. The bottom line is that the current market for cryptocurrencies is out of control and essentially unregulated.

2018 was a transformational year for regulation of established cryptocurrency exchanges. At least two ICOs, **Coinbase** and **Ivy Koin**, have approached federal regulators about the possibility of obtaining banking licenses.

Coinbase operates the largest cryptocurrency exchange as measured by trading volume. Ivy Koin is a cryptocurrency payments startup. After meetings with federal regulators[37], both companies are seeking bank charters, while recognizing that this direction would significantly open them up to regulatory oversight.

Coinbase only admitted that the firm is "committed to working closely with state regulators to insure that we are properly licensed for the products and services we offer." Ivy Coin, on the other hand, is working closely with banks rather than trying to become one.

The concept of applying for bank charters is relatively new in the cryptocurrency sector, but it has promise. Acquiring any federal license could help these companies acquire major investors such as hedge funds. A charter could lead to companies in this sector providing custody or payments services *even if their deposits are not insured*.

---

[37] Coinbase founders met with the US Office of the Comptroller of the Currency, while Ivy Koin execs met with officials at the FDIC.

The movement is toward pre-emptive federal regulation across state lines. However, there is no coherent or consistent direction among U.S. government agencies.

The Securities and Exchange Commission (SEC) issues warnings to potential investors about high risk and volatility.

The Commodity Futures Trading Commission (CFTC) is the first authority to allow cryptocurrency derivatives to trade publicly.

Secretary of State Steve Mnuchin prefers "minted" fiat currency to avoid money-laundering activities.

Among the states, there are inconsistent and sometimes vague licensing requirements for exchanges and payment services. Federal regulations might put an umbrella over these regulations.

Chapter 4. Blockchain Technology

Trust, Consensus, Immutable

> **Industrial Revolution 4.0**
>
> We are witnessing the emergence of the fourth industrial revolution. It is characterized by *distributed* technology that blurs the lines among physical, digital and biological spheres to completely disrupt industries and commerce all over the world. This revolution is transforming production, management and governance systems.

The **blockchain** concept originated in 1991 when Stuart Haber and W. Scott Stornetta described work contained within a cryptographically secured chain of blocks. In 1992, they incorporated Merkle trees[38] into the design allowing several documents to be collected into a block. This was the technology used by Nakamoto in 2009 to "mine" the first Bitcoins.

Blockchain, the technology that underlies all cryptocurrencies, has developed over the last decade into one of today's most promising and ground-breaking technologies with the potential to impact every industry and disrupt commerce.

---

[38] A Merkle tree is a hierarchical structure in which every leaf node has a label (index) which is the cryptographic hash of its "child".

The most promising characteristic of blockchain technology is that it elevates trust to a level far beyond that in conventional transactions.

A concise definition of trust is that it is a confident relationship with the unknown. Blockchain technology can be trusted because it has the inherent potential to create a *permanent* public and immutable record of ownership of every asset.

The trust inherent in blockchains creates verifiable and immutable relationships. It democratizes the way transaction data is stored. It is proof of ownership and eliminates the need for audits. It can be applied to *any* asset.

When a blockchain transaction is initiated, algorithms within a network of computers ("nodes") validate that the transaction is capable of succeeding *(i.e., there is enough currency)*. Then the record of the transaction is added to an encrypted chain of other parties' related transactions. This chain is immutable; no change can be made on any node unless it is verified on all nodes.

In Rachel Botsman's enlightening book **Who Can You Trust**, she points out that on the Pacific Island of Yap, where women frequently wear only grass skirts, the trusted currency for transactions is the ancient stone money known as the 'fei'. Economists look at this currency in the quest to answer a fundamental question: "What is money?".

In traditional banking and investing systems, intermediaries such as banks, government agencies and service organizations are required to enable and validate the integrity of a transaction. This slows the process and is costly.

It is estimated that, if middlemen could be eliminated, consumers would save up to $16 billion a year in banking, insurance and processing fees. In addition to savings, blockchains reduce the lifecycle of a trade from days to minutes *(or even seconds)*.

Blockchains reduce or eliminate settlement and compliance costs as well as cross-border costs for international trades. They can also be the repository for an immutable database of passports, drivers' licenses and other means of identification.

Companies like Digital Asset Holdings are emerging throughout the world as service providers for the distributed platforms that process these rapid transactions and build blockchains. The result is an "immutable audit trail" with transparency and traceability. The traceability concept applies not only to currency, but also to products with compliance requirements *(i.e., lot numbers)*, to monitoring products in transit, and to "smart" contracts.

How does it work?

Blockchain technology is decentralized, requires validation by consensus, and is immutable. Each block is timestamped, and each transaction is encrypted with a hash identifier.

To understand how blockchains can be used in commerce, let's look at how a broker now sells a home, and how a home could be sold within a blockchain structure.

Buying a home is the biggest investment that most people will make in their lifetimes. However, there have been few technological advances to expedite the transaction and make it more secure for buyers, sellers, brokers and lenders.

The traditional real estate transaction typically involves several tedious steps:

- Open escrow.
- Title search and insurance.
- Use an Attorney to assure compliance.
- Pre-approved the mortgage.
- Negotiate closing costs.
- Home inspection.
- Pest inspection.
- Renegotiate when inspections reveal flaws.
- Lock in an interest rate.
- Remove contingencies.
- Fund the escrow.
- Final walkthrough.
- Sign the Documents.

What if the real estate transaction could be absolutely trusted with guaranteed auditability and privacy? With blockchain technology, the middleman *(the escrow or title company)* is no longer a part of a transaction. Instead, all components of the transaction are contained within an encrypted distributed database with proven authenticity. Transfer of ownership can take place immediately upon payment without the need for third-party verification.

To further the real estate analogy, you could rent an apartment on a blockchain service by paying in either cryptocurrency or dollars. You would get a receipt from the landlord which is retained in a virtual "smart" contract.

The landlord promises to deliver a digital entry key to the renter by a specified date. If the key does not arrive by that date, the blockchain releases a refund. If the key is sent on or before the contractual rental date, the blockchain releases the key to the tenant and the rental fee to the landlord. During this entire process, the smart contract cannot be altered.

Blockchain technology shields all parties from any exposure to fraud. When all documents related to ownership of property are secured within a chain, forgery or modification of these documents is not possible. If the property owner want to rent the property, "sub"-agreements can be easily added to the chain.

A blockchain is a ledger of facts, distributed across a decentralized peer-to-peer (P2P) network. These P2P networks resolve conflicts without human interference.

Without blockchains, conflicts can occur. For example, if Alice has $120 in her checking account and tries to send $100 checks to both Bob and Charlie, then whoever receives the check first will cash it. If Bob receives the check before Charlie and cashes it, Charlie's attempt to cash his check will result in Alice's account being overdrawn; she will probably be charged an overdraft fee and Charlie's check will be returned. Software developers call this the **double spend problem** as depicted on the next page.

The double-spend problem

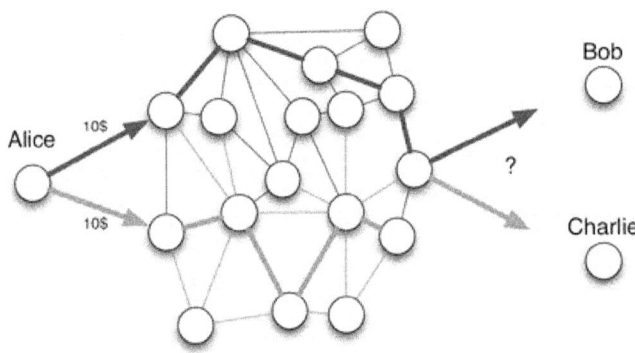

In order to guarantee integrity over a peer-to-peer network, all parties must agree on the **facts**. Any conflict gets resolved in a **consensus** system. Developers of blockchain software for providers of distributed ledger technology (DLT) services construct algorithms that insure **proof-of-work** consensus.

In a DLT network, all facts are grouped into a single chain of blocks, which are replicated through the entire network. *Pending* blocks can't be added to the chain until they are confirmed.

Pending facts in blocks remain local and the algorithm repeatedly encrypts each block with a unique "hash tag". The block is then digitally chained to all other nodes in the network.

Once all nodes confirm that the facts in a new block are correct, then the block is added to all nodes in the chain, and linked back to the previous block. This immensely repetitive process consumes enormous amounts of electricity *(or battery power)* throughout the network and is the most critical detriment to implementing DLT as a service. However, as computing performance increases dramatically, it is expected that this roadblock will be overcome.

These hash-tags are not random, and it is very unlikely that any software could surreptitiously generate a random key to validate a block. This is because blockchain consensus software repeatedly generates a 250-byte *(character)* hashtag until the resulting tag contains 10 or more zeroes following the decimal point. Confirmed blocks get published to the chain at a fixed time

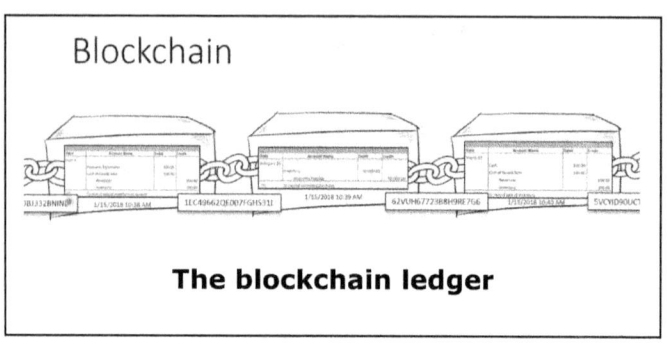

interval *(in Bitcoin, blocks are published every 10 minutes)*.

The process of looking for blocks that are gems *(confirmed)* within a sea of pending blocks is called **mining**.

Blockchain technology has three distinct forms of operating software, depending upon its user community:

❖ Public – usually underpinning Bitcoin and other cryptocurrencies, typically used for cryptocurrency exchange.

- Private – technology tools used within a corporate entity such as IBM or Walmart.
- Consortium – requires the consensus of several independent entities, as used in smart contracts.

Blockchain as a Service

Because the underlying software platform can only be produced by a consortium of developers with great intelligence, skills, creativity and lots of money, only giant companies with dedicated research and development (R&D) teams, or startups backed by venture capitalists, have the resources to build **Blockchain as a Service (BaaS)** platforms. It is expected that the blockchain technology market worldwide will expand to $7.7 Billion by 2024.

The BaaS model allows businesses of all sizes to access and use the technology without a major in-house investment. Businesses will typically use a blockchain provider's service where they can develop customized applications or license existing blockchain applications.

Many early Blockchain Solution Providers (**BSP**s) have joined the **Hyperledger Project** so that they can collaborate on the harnessing of this new-age technology and promulgate standards for the businesses and institutions *(such as the IRS or Passport Agencies)* that adopt it. Because this is an open-source platform, it can seamlessly integrate with other emerging technologies like artificial intelligence and machine learning.

Enterprises today with huge distribution challenges are turning to BSPs to provide customized platforms that support distributed ledger technology. Early solution providers of democratized blockchain technology are Microsoft, IBM, Deloitte, Baidu and Tencent.

Microsoft's Azure is a cloud-based service that provides a platform for building, testing and implementing customized distributed applications within a global network of Microsoft data centers. Azure provides a broad array of hosted services "in the clouds" that enables enterprises to host web and email servers, databases, and file storage without capital expenditures. Azure is the platform upon which other enterprises can facilitate distributed ledger technology to support their operations.

IBM's Blockchain Platform claimed in 2018 to be the only fully integrated enterprise-ready platform designed to support multi-institution business networks. They assure their users that all activity within the network is secure and has the consensus of all nodes, while providing an immutable audit trail of all activity.

IBM's technology is built on open-source Hyperledger software available from the Linux Foundation. It's customers can easily develop a blockchain ecosystem within a cloud-based platform. It is a flexible software-as-a-service (SaaS) offering delivered through the IBM Cloud.

Enterprises that subscribe to IBM Blockchain can integrate open-source developer tools to produce customized blockchain code as well as smart contracts. Collaboration tools are provided that include staff activities, integrated notifications and secure signature collection for sign-off on policies. Subscribers can significantly reduce development time.

The network itself has guaranteed availability and security, with frequent blockchain network updates. IBM's BaaS is a tamper-proof distributed ledger within which any company can establish a trusted network where data can be freely shared *only* among credentialed members.

IBM's technology is already being used to track high-end products like diamonds and fine art from origin to consumer. The goal, obviously, is to prevent theft and counterfeiting.

In January 2017, **Deloitte** announced that it had established a blockchain laboratory in New York. According to Joe Guastella, an executive, the purpose of the laboratory is "to support Deloitte's clients and practitioners across industries in harnessing the opportunities and capabilities that blockchain technology has to offer."

An example of how entrepreneurs can transform an ICO into a BaaS platform is the **Telegram** Group, founded by two Russian brothers, Pavel and Nikolai Durov. The platform was initially intended to operate as an encrypted messaging service free from government surveillance.

Pavel Durov is the face of Telegram. He founded VKontakte *(known in Russia as VK)* as a social media website that became the 17th most trafficked website in the world. VK was attractive to Russians because of its *encrypted* text-messaging service. Exposed to controversy from the Russian government, the brothers fled to Berlin, Singapore and London before finally settling in Dubai to run Telegram.

The brothers then decided to establish their own cryptocurrency, called a **gram**, in order to connect their technology to a broader market. Initially, they expected to raise $1.2 billion from their ICO, split evenly between rounds of public and private fundraising.

Instead, in February 2018, the Durovs reported to the SEC that they had raised $1.7 billion from two rounds of fundraising. Telegram's investors were required to be *accredited*, which meant they must either exceed minimum income requirements or have a net worth of at least $1 million.

Telegram's plans are to build an online services platform based upon blockchain technology that could "become a Visa/Mastercard alternative for a new decentralized economy." The objective of this project, called the **Telegram Open Network**, is to provide a service monetized by grams, while continuing to maintain their encrypted messenger service, which has about 200 million users.

This venture has received kudos from privacy advocates, but its critics say that this platform is really intended to be a secure communications and exchange platform for militants and terrorists.

It is certain that within the next 20 years, **Blockchain as a**

Service (**BaaS**) will be pervasive for most commercial transactions.

Smart Contracts

In 1994, Nick Szabo, a respected computer scientist and legal scholar, realized that a decentralized and distributed ledger could be the foundation for *smart* self-executing contracts. These contracts could be digitized, stored in a distributed database, and propagated throughout the network of computer nodes within the blockchain service.

This concept can be applied to *any* transaction between two parties. Today, much time and effort is consumed by CPAs, lawyers, sales people and other professionals interpreting and enforcing contractual agreements. These "professional services" cost time and money and do not guarantee trust and immutability.

Smart Contracts are a computerized protocol based upon algorithms that digitally facilitate, verify and enforce the negotiation or performance of a contract. A smart contract encapsulates the performance of credible transactions without requiring third party verification and audit. These transactions are traceable, irreversible and distributed among all involved parties, who each have access to only that data which applies to them.

Smart Contracts facilitate the exchange of anything of value *(money, property, shares etc.)* in a transparent, conflict-free manner while avoiding the services of a middleman. They are comprised of (1) an agreement between parties, (2) a triggering event and (3) ongoing regulation.

Wallets

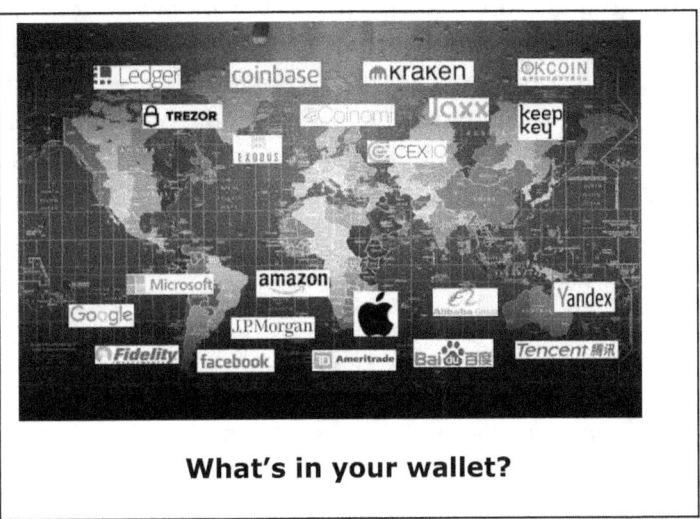

What's in your wallet?

Most distributed ledger transactions today require that a cryptocurrency exchange occur between two parties. Not only is a Blockchain Solution Provider required to effect the transaction and build the blockchain, but also a third-party like one of those shown above is needed to transfer the cryptocurrency *(or currency)* from the buyer to the seller. If the two parties are transferring **cryptocurrency**, they both need a wallet.

A *digital* wallet is an app on an electronic device or provided by an online service that facilitates an electronic transaction. An individual's bank account can be linked to the digital wallet for both purchases and receipts. A digital wallet is used to store, send and receive cryptocurrency.

Cryptocurrency itself is not "stored" in the wallet. Instead, a private encrypted digital key known to only the owner of the wallet is stored electronically in the owner's device. This is connected to a digital public key which is connected to a balance of cryptocurrency in the owner's wallet. Because of the separation of these keys into private and public, any transaction that uses the public key will not necessarily know the identity of the holder of the private key. The wallet itself contains the personal ledger of all the owner's transactions.

There are services available for specific cryptocurrencies such at **Bitcoin Core Wallet**, **Litecoin Core** or **Ethereum Wallet**.

There are also universal wallet services such as HolyTransaction and Coinomi that will hold many, but not all, cryptocurrencies.

Be aware that some providers or apps may be offering malware that could subject you to identity theft. Never trust wallet software that comes from a source that you do not trust!

Most wallets can be downloaded. However, there are several types of wallets and you should select the type that best suits your lifestyle.

Desktop wallets. This is the most common type of wallet and runs on a desktop personal computer. It connects the client *(you)* to the distributed ledger service.

Mobile wallets. These wallets are run from a mobile device like a smartphone[39].

Online wallets. These wallets are hosted or web-based. You don't download the app. Instead, your wallet's data is hosted on

---

[39] Some wallets are both a desktop application and a mobile app.

a server.

Hardware wallets. These wallets are dedicated hardware devices like a USB jump drive that securely holds cryptocurrency.

Paper Wallets. You have the capability to print a QR code[40] for both your public and your private key. This lets you avoid storing digital data.

---

[40] A QR code is matrix barcode on paper or a device that is readable with an optical reader or the camera on a mobile device.

Professionals

Within the next decade, blockchains will have transformed the way accountants, CPAs and lawyers do business and they will probably eliminate the need for tax preparers or auditors.

Professionals will be forced to adopt this technology and adapt to the peer-to-peer networks that blockchain facilitates. When intermediaries such as banks are eliminated and a permanent public record of all transactions is available, accountants will no longer be needed to reconcile bank statements and "bookkeeping" will not be required. CPAs will no longer be hired as auditors. Tax preparers will be out of work.

To avoid unemployment, professionals will need to transform their practices away from compliance, which is already built into blockchains, and toward helping their clients grow their businesses and increase their profits by depending upon an infrastructure wherein financial databases are analyzed and these professionals become significant contributors to forecasting the direction of their clients' companies.

Consultants that embrace this technology will mentor their clients by leading them into adapting it for their own enterprises, with a guaranteed outcome of reducing costs of maintaining and reconciling ledgers. This will have a significant impact on the way accounting firms structure their engagement letters.

Chapter 5. Disrupting Commerce

Today, blockchain technology is disrupting world commerce. Distributed ledgers, constructed as blockchains and frequently updated, with encrypted immutable transaction data available and pervasive throughout world commerce.

DLT applications have captured all the wonder of this Blockchain Revolution. These platforms are empowered with machine learning, predictive analysis, and constantly changing decision-making based upon a universe of available analytics.

The blockchain ledger replicates all historical transactions across millions of computers. This prevents a single user from tampering with history, since all records within this vast ledger are imputable and permanently linked to each other.

Information can only be added to a blockchain, and it is unalterable. A distributed ledger transaction does not require any intermediary, such as a bank or an agent to adjudicate it.

This technological shift in the way business is conducted throughout the world will insure that all transactions are transparent and incorruptible, and embodied with trust.

Initial deployments of blockchain technology were founded in financial services. We are now witnessing an evolution that is transforming society, business and government throughout the world.

Any industry that deals with massive databases driven by transactions will likely be disrupted by blockchain technology and distributed ledgers. As of early 2018, nearly 15% of financial institutions were either exploring or using blockchain technology. Blockchains have vast potential to disrupt commerce and society even when completely separated from cryptocurrency. It is expected that all industries will fully incorporate blockchains by 2020.

Thought leader Martin Ford, in a TED talk on disruptions to occupations in 2018, predicted that this disruption will significantly drive changes in the types of jobs that are available globally. in his opinion, this forecasts the inevitability of a basic minimum income that must protect all of the populace.

On the following pages, we will examine many of the industries that will be disrupted and transformed, along with snapshots of enterprises that have embraced this technology.

Disrupted and Transformed Industries

Identity Management

Cyber attacks in the last decade have stolen the identities of millions of people throughout the world. For many, it has devastated their credit ratings or wiped out their savings.

A blockchain ledger can prevent identity theft by connecting users of services such as banks and ecommerce sites where personal and account information is stored, most often with insufficient security.

Protection of personal data within blockchains can be fueled by encrypted **SSID**[41] access tokens. These tokens are objects which define the security context of a thread of data related to an entity. The features of an SSID are:

- A token "key", which can be freely traded.
- An identity wallet.
- Integration with a payment service.
- Facilitation of setup of new accounts.
- Secure and private management of documents *(such as passports and drivers licenses)*.
- Isolation of all SSIDs on the user's device unless the user chooses to share some or all of the information with others.

A leader in this technology is **Selfkey**. This blockchain-based public self-sovereigned identity service allows any company to own and manage their digital identity and their cryptocurrency portfolio. It eliminates paper-based documents and manual filing systems. Selfkey enables identity wallets with encrypted SSIDs that can be seamlessly integrated into financial, immigration and cryptocurrency exchanges. The vision of the Selfkey community is a free world where identified transactions in blockchains are

[41] **S**elf-**S**overeign **ID**entity

secure, private and without a centralized issuing authority.

Music and Publishing

Blockchains will soon enable artists and writers to be paid directly by their fans, bypassing agents and publishing houses. Licenses for their work will be executed as immutable smart contracts. A universal distributed database will catalog all of their work with immutable copyrights, thus diminishing or eliminating current practices of streaming songs without royalties being paid.

Without DLT, it is very difficult for unrecognized writers to publish their work. Either they resort to self-publishing, which is most often not lucrative, or they go through a firewall of literary agents hoping that they can somehow interest them in passing their work on to publishers.

Now writers have another option. They can go to a platform called **Authorship**[42], an ICO in January 2018, and democratize the publishing of their book.

Authorship's decentralized platform brings authors, publishers, readers and even translators together with an **ATS** token.

The ATS cryptocurrency is built upon an Ethereum platform and is a unit of exchange. Any transaction related to the sale of a publication in this network results in the exchange of ATS tokens. Readers can spend the ATS tokens in their digital wallets acquired from the **HitBTC** exchange, to purchase other books.

Blockchains enable person-to-person networks where musicians can release their music directly to their fans. Two popular startups now operate in this space, **Ujo Music** and **Mycelia**.

---

[42] In August, 2014, Google ended support for the authorship platform.

Imogen Heap is a Grammy-winning British singer and songwriter who launched **Ujo Music** in 2015. This blockchain was based on Ethereum for the purpose of marketing her song "Tiny Human" for 45 pence per download. This led to the creation of Mycelia.

Mycelia, also founded by Imogen Heap, is a collective of music creators, industry professionals and music lovers. Content creators in this space protect their copyrights and receive direct payment for their work. Blockchains contain auditable and immutable records of who created and owns an asset. These blockchains enable peer-to-peer transactions in several popular cryptocurrencies, resulting in complete transparency, automated execution of royalty rights, and direct payments to copyright holders.

Retailers

Brick and mortar stores as well as e-commerce web sites such as Amazon will not need to record sales and receive payments as they do now. Instead, BaaS apps will use decentralized distributed ledgers to connect buyers and sellers without a middleman or service fees. Trusted transactions will be managed within smart contracts which insure consumer trust and the security, accuracy and immutability of exchanges between buyer and seller.

There are several blockchain partner solutions for eCommerce platforms. Most notable are **Kaleido**, **Sawtooth** and **R3**.

Sawtooth is a modular enterprise tool for building, deploying and managing distributed ledgers. It is not directed at any specific industry. It is open source software which can be downloaded from GitHub. Extensive documentation is provided for application developers, including modular building blocks and sample applications. Once developed, there is an extensive network of vendors who offer blockchain products and services.

Kaleido is a blockchain service (SaaS) that supports the deployment and operation of private blockchain networks. Essentially, it eliminates the development stage for its users.

Kaleido accelerates the journey from modeling and experimentation to pilot projects and on to full deployment. It is a collaboration between **ConsenSys** and **Amazon** web services intended to simplify adoption of private blockchains by eCommerce enterprises. It is in the infant stages of its offering *(in 2018)* and has not yet proven to be viable. Their challenge is connecting public and private chains within a single network.

R3 is a distributed ledger platform directed toward the world's largest financial institutions. It claims to meet the highest standards of the banking industry. This finance platform is now in the pilot stage and has not yet been deployed. The goal for R3 is to provide a "fully operable" open-source financial network built upon R3's distributed ledger technology product **Corda** and delivered over **TradeIX**'s open TIX trading platform.

Deployment of most of these DLT platforms has not yet arrived. Kaleido, mentioned above, seems to be the most viable offering *(in mid-2018)*. Amazon is also working with blockchain startups, offering dedicated technical support and the infrastructure to build upon. Expect most of these deployments by 2020.

Real Estate

In my introduction to blockchain technology, I gave an example of how a real estate sale might be recorded within a blockchain. In today's world of exploding home prices, particularly in technology centers such as Silicon Valley, workers in high-tech companies are moving toward long-term rentals. Many of these younger generation professionals don't have the time or knowledge to find a suitable home, enter into a complicated agreement, or agree to pay a security deposit <u>that is recoverable</u>. Several blockchain-based companies have been established that attempt to manage rentals, but they are saddled with many problems.

Blockchains for real estate sales have been far more successful. An example of an ICO supporting *commercial* property sales is **Atlant**. This is a rapidly growing blockchain platform based upon the Goodmall cryptocurrency.

Owners of high-priced commercial property list their asset on the Atlant site with an asking price. Atlant verifies that the property meets all of its stringent requirements for listing and that the title is clean and is not encumbered by debt. Very often the intended buyer of the property will form a special purpose vehicle (SPV) which is a unique type of corporation used to buy and sell commercial property.

Atlant then tokenizes the SPV, establishing a listing price in tokens, and places a Property Token Offering on its trading platform. Investors around the world can purchase tokens and acquire partial ownership of the asset. This continues until the asset is fully funded, at which time the equivalent of the sales price in Goodmall tokens is transferred in tokens to the former owner. Owners of Goodmall tokens not only profit from their properties' rental income, but they also monetize changes in token prices in a secondary market where investors can buy or sell a percentage of a certain property by trading in Goodmall tokens.

Smart Contracts

Challenges In the supply chain industry are focused upon reducing costs of distributing products to retailers and customers while improving the efficiency of their operations.

Smart contracts bring order to this chaos. Early in the chain, these blockchains make "just in time" manufacturing possible based upon the number of orders in the pipeline by producing purchase orders for precisely what is needed to fulfill the bills of materials for open orders. This reduces the inventory in their warehouses as well as their backlog of unfulfilled orders.

All transactions related to inventory are recorded in a decentralized distributed ledger. This database lends itself to analysis of products or components at company, industry or demographic levels. Future costs of components and labor can be reduced as a result of this analysis. It also lends itself to monitoring waste and emissions at every point in the supply chain. A supply chain blockchain will no doubt improve transparency, trust and predictability by allowing users to track where a shipment is at any point in time. Using blockchain technology to enable instant settlement of transactions will reduce trade disputes, particularly as it relates to world trade and shipping.

In January 2018, IBM and Maersk announced a joint venture to digitize supply chains and track cargo in real time. This blockchain-based electronic shipping system is not tied to any cryptocurrency. The system is intended to replace current EDI[43] and paper-based systems with a single view into a virtual dashboard where the shipping information for all parties involved is accessible by viewing the contents of this chain. Security is significantly improved by double encryption of all GPS-guided and scanned location detail within the entire blockchain. A real-time <u>audit trail for regulators is</u> constantly updated, and visibility is

[43] Electronic Data Interchange

significantly improved.

Government

Perhaps the most universal application of distributed ledgers will be how governments embrace it throughout the world. Blockchains may have a greater impact on society than what transpired in the early days of the internet.

In light of the events in the 2016 presidential election, where voting decisions driven by fake social media posts were manipulated, there will be significant movement toward blockchain technology to secure future elections, and audit all voting activity in real time. It is expected that blockchain platforms will ultimately be pervasive for use in voter identification, registration, and secure counting of votes. This immutable record will be publicly available.

The chronology of ownership *(titles)* of all real estate within a jurisdiction could be managed within a distributed ledger. Blockchain technology will revolutionize government record keeping. If all public records were maintained in a distributed ledger, any authorized citizen could access records such as proof of title, tax returns, and utility payments. The public could have access to government budgets and spending. The possibilities worldwide are unlimited.

There is increasing evidence of identity theft, as well as hacking of government databases of drivers' licenses, passports and employee IDs.

In 2017, thousands of passports were lost or stolen, resulting in an underground market for counterfeit passports in almost all countries. It is well known that manual passport checks at long lines in customs checkpoints are, at best, inefficient and, at worst, non-productive. Encrypted passports in blockchains could be digitized and stored on a passenger's device along with biometric information, significantly reducing the bottlenecks at customs checkpoints.

In January 2018, a bill was introduced in Florida to allow the state to implement a digital driver's license program. This program would include a "digital proof of driver license" component within the blockchain.

Nearly one-fifth of the world's population have no official identification such as a birth certificate or social security card. In underdeveloped countries, many people cannot prove their identity. This results in diminished human rights and exploitation of refugees, making them vulnerable to human trafficking schemes. One theory to counter this crisis is the "Humanized Internet", conceived by Monique Morrow, a technology leader in the IEEE, in March of 2017. Her plan is to offer a blockchain based Identity as a Service (IaaS) platform to counter this crisis.

Healthcare

In the United States, the healthcare industry contributed to 20% of the economy in 2017. Pharmaceutical companies are continually confronted to make prescription medicines affordable, while the insurance industry is subject to widespread fraud and counterfeit claims.

Distributed data for medical records is already evolving. DLT is currently employed to order and refill prescriptions and to process claims. It will be used increasingly over the next few years for tracking research and development of new drugs, and for testing with study groups comprised of selected volunteers throughout the world.

Distributed databases of welfare, unemployment, and Social Security benefits will be widely utilized to prevent fraud and to confirm identities. It is possible that these databases could be the basis for guaranteeing a minimum basic income for everyone, thereby reducing the number of people on welfare.

The primary problem in the healthcare industry is storage of, and access to, patient data. Secure storage and access to this data is fraught with problems, the most costly of which is fraudulent claims.

In developing nations, healthcare systems are typically legacy systems, which are decades old, inaccurate and not part of an international database. If blockchain technology were ubiquitous throughout the world, a universal and immutable database of patient data, medical procedures, prescriptions and an accurate audit trail of claims would exist.

The distributed ledger for this industry would create a common universal database of comprehensive patient health information that doctors, providers and first responders could access no matter what electronic medical system (EMS) they used, insuring security and privacy for all patients.

Healthcare Rallies for Blockchain, a study by IBM of 200 healthcare executives, found that 16% of payers and providers are expected to have a commercial blockchain solution at scale by the end of 2017. This has been achieved.

The widespread use of blockchains in the healthcare industry is expected to emerge in the following areas:

- Claims and billing management
- Drug research and development
- Supply chain integrity
- Compliance and traceability
- Medical Research
- Data security and patient privacy

Insurance and Risk

BaaS platforms can enhance the assessment and analysis of risk for insurance services, and facilitate the concept within the industry of "pay-as-you-need". Homeowners who offer rentals through VRBO or Airbnb, concerned that claims resulting from damage or losses by their renters will not be covered in standard homeowners' policies, are turning to specialized add-on coverage through providers such as **HomeAway Assure** and **CBIZ**.

The insurance industry gains by employing blockchains for:

- Improving customer engagement by digitally storing policyholder information in a distributed ledger.
- Improving fraud detection with transparency of transactions and identification of multiple claims.
- Automation of claims processing across a distributed ledger.
- New product development as a result of analysis of a vast distributed database of claims processing.

The greatest concern for insurers is uncertainty of the direction of regulations. The industry wants confirmation that blockchain activity is reliable, and that smart contracts are legal in the courts.

Insurers want minimum standards and processes established for smart contracts. In late 2017, the world's leading IT research and advisory company Gartner positioned blockchain "close to the peak of inflated expectations". Insurers that adopt blockchain now will only know in three to five years if they were successful.

The benefits for the insurance industry are uncertain and difficult to measure. It could reduce the human resources devoted to claims processing. Filers of claims within their smart contracts might receive payments before the damage is fully assessed. However, claims adjusters are still needed to evaluate claims and assess damages before settling a claim. Blockchains would certainly reduce overhead related to manual data entry of claims.

For new customers, blockchains will be invaluable. Smart contracts will be linked to all known information about the applicant and automatically calculate the premium based upon risk assessment of the applicant's health, driving records, work history and demographics.

The enthusiasm about this breakthrough technology is sometimes exaggerated and could bias an objective evaluation about whether or not to invest. It is evident that blockchain introduces a radical transformation in transactions and contracts, and we need to prepare for these changes by learning all we can about blockchain.

Charities

Blockchain-as-a-service (**BaaS**) is becoming more popular as a means of tracking pledges and donations to charities. Blockchains insure that donations are distributed to the intended recipients. Blockchains insure that charitable institutions are legitimate and are performing their stated mission within the law.

These services work best when the technology links blockchains to specific cryptocurrencies. There is an evolving trend toward leveraging cryptocurrencies for philanthropic purposes. Even Red Cross and United Way have adopted the technology. Online wallets allow charities to accept cryptocurrencies from donors and exchange them for fiat currencies such as the dollar at the current exchange rate. These donations are tax deductible and currently offer donors the additional benefit of avoiding capital gains taxes[44].

In January 2018, **AidCoin** issued an ICO claiming to be the most simple and transparent solution for efficient donations. At this time, the non-profit sector had a reputation for corruption and gross inefficiencies. AidCoin hopes to overcome the public perception of a sector that lacks transparency and accountability.

Consequences of scandals in this century are alarming. In the United States in 2017, 52% of charities were unfunded due to difficulty in finding donors and inability to meet the demand for their services.

AidCoin professes that, with DLT, donors will be able to track how money is allocated and deployed. Trust is restored to the process since no record on the blockchain can be destroyed or altered. It brings traceability, transparency and accountability to the sector.

---

[44] Regulators are considering imposing capital gain taxes on the fluctuations of the underlying cryptocurrencies.

BaaS providers like AidCoin reduce costs in the supply chain since government agencies and banks are no longer middlemen in the process and no credit or debit fees are imposed by clearing houses. If predetermined restrictions and conditions are not fulfilled, smart contracts will insure that donors get refunds or that funds are redirected to more pressing causes such as natural disasters. Furthermore, while traditional donations over $5,000 require an appraisal, blockchain donations are exempt since they are transparent and publicly traded.

AidCoin is seen as bringing effective altruism to donors and recipients. It helps charities by reducing costs and increasing efficiency and bringing transparency, visibility and auditability to charitable projects.

Financial Services

It is expected that access to financial services via blockchain technology will become available to those who don't currently have the ability or means to use traditional banking, especially those in underdeveloped third world nations. Many banks, including giant Bank of America, are now adopting blockchain technology.

We are witnessing an explosion of applications in the financial industry that ennervate the global economy with rapid, secure and private transactions. Traditional banking lacks fairness. Customers gain very little from their interaction with banks, and this has triggered a reduction in the number of physical branches while increasing the use of ATMs and online or mobile banking.

Cryptocurrencies on blockchain platforms are transforming traditional payment systems. Today, almost anyone can start a payments enterprise with incorruptible distributed ledgers that require no regulatory oversight. This puts transactional authority back into the consumer's hands and eliminates exorbitant service fees, interest payments and middlemen.

To enliven this movement, two ventures have come to the forefront with unique approaches: **Ripple** and **OmiseGo**.

Ripple's RippleNet connects banks, payment providers and digital asset exchanges as a service for transferring funds globally. It is a real-time settlement system built upon distributed open source protocol and a cryptocurrency aptly named the Ripple, abbreviated as **XRP**. It has been increasingly adopted by banks and payment networks because of trust in its settlement infrastructure. This advanced technology circumvents reliance on centralized cryptocurrency exchanges, uses far less electricity than Bitcoin transfers and processes transactions remarkably faster. It enables instant and direct transfer of money between two parties, avoids the fees and wait times imposed by traditional correspondent banks, and any currency *(or even airline miles)* may be exchanged.

OmiseGo is based solely on Ethereum and offers a full range of financial and payment services to any individual. This platform focuses on the underdeveloped world where many people do not have bank accounts. It is an open payment platform and a decentralized exchange. Its token **OMG** is one of the highest market cap Ethereum projects in the world. It's unique approach is that OMG is traded as a "currency pair" within the exchange and the token is *paired* with one or more currencies such as the dollar or the euro.

Network Support

Product support centers *(typically called Information Technology, or IT)* are creating blockchain-based networks that employ public ledgers to support devices and products across vast networks without human oversight. Centralized network support centers and IT organizations can be eliminated. Within the blockchain network, devices can communicate directly with each other to update software, repair hardware, analyze "bug" reports, and monitor energy usage across vast private or government networks.

Blockchain technology, coupled with artificial intelligence, opens the door for our smart devices to be interconnected on the world wide web, sometimes even leaving the owner of the devices completely in the dark while it recognizes situations and responds to them. With blockchains recording all events securely and instantly, we are of course exposed to potential security and transactional situations that, in some cases, will be unwanted, unplanned or even dangerous. This technology often uses radio frequency identification (RFID) to detect extraordinary situations or the need for scheduled servicing, appropriate responses, and encryption of the results of its activity in a blockchain.

Crowdfunding

Crowdfunding is the practice of funding a project or venture by raising small amounts of money from a large number of people. Activity is typically on the internet. Crowdfunding brings together individuals who fund entrepreneurs with a promising concept or venture. Presently these ventures are funded in dollars in the US and there is typically no promise of repayment. Today there are emerging decentralized ICO platforms where entrepreneurs and artists can launch their ventures on independent blockchains without risk or debt.

Komodo provides startups and artists with the two models for generating their own blockchains.

One model is an open-source "toolkit" that jumpstarts their projects. A chain-generator "mines" the unique coins, security services are imbedded, and rules and consensus mechanisms are developed. The result is a person-to-person (P2P) risk-free crowdfunding campaign.

The **Premier Partner** model brings expert support and services to the venture. The platform is co-marketed and there is dedicated assistance during the launching of the campaign.

Early adopter **Ultrum** claims that "It just took 3 simple steps to build our independent blockchain, explorer and OOT token integration in Komodo's multi wallet and decentralized exchange".

Kickstarter focuses on funding for the arts. It is a crowdfunding platform with a mission to "help bring creative projects to life". Launched in April 2009, Kickstarter has received almost $2 billion in pledges from 9.4 million participants and has funded over 250,000 ventures.

This app circumvents traditional avenues of investment by requiring project creators to set deadlines and minimum funding goals. If a goal is not met by the deadline, no funds are collected, and pledges recorded in assurance contracts[45] are cancelled.

[45] Assurance contracts are a form of smart contracts that facilitate

The **Elixir** crowdfunding platform is based upon smart contracts that manage startup projects in almost any industry. The Ethereum token is the exchange medium. Unlike Kickstarter, both a minimum and a maximum goal can be set for each project, but it is not required. The creator of each project can specify a "host cut", which is a percentage of the total funding that the host will receive.

Elixir is a blockchain platform that allows users to create and request loans, make payments and crowdfund venture projects. It is a true P2P *(peer-to-peer)* experience, with incentives for borrowers to repay their loans and for lenders to share in the profits *(or assets)* of these ventures.

---

voluntary creation of public goods tied to specific funding goals.

Ridesharing

Blockchain technology is emerging throughout the auto industry and is certain to disrupt the ridesharing model. Startup P2P services such as **Uber** and **Lyft** enable carpoolers to make digital payments for their rides in tokens without a central authority. This distributed ledger platform enables users to connect transparently using Ethereum as the unit of exchange.

Because these services prevent driver bonuses, it levels the playing field. On a broader scale, the smart contract between driver and rider secures terms and conditions without intermediaries. Drivers will use their e-wallets to pay for parking, highway tolls and charging of electric vehicles, and riders will use their e-wallets to pay fares.

This technology is expected to disrupt Uber and Lyft. Instead of an intermediary to clear payments and match drivers with riders, driver profiles would be posted on a universal blockchain, and the blockchain itself would filter for the best driver for each ride request in a peer-to-peer network. Riders could post reviews on the blockchain, improving or hurting the reputation and success of available drivers.

Logistics - the Ultimate Use of Blockchain Technology

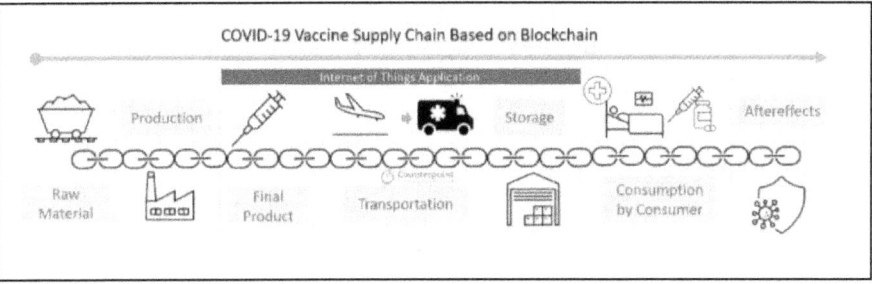

In December 2020, The U.S. Food and Drug Administration issued an emergency authortization for the use of a vaccine for the prevention of the COVID-19 virus. Operation Warp Speed's logistics plan for distribution of the vaccine was under the direction of four-star General Gustave Perna. General Perna had previously served for two years as the Army's Deputy Chief of Staff and as commanding general of the U. S. Army's Materiel Command in 2016. This authorization launched an unprecedented logistics operation, the largest in the history of logistics.

Operation Warp Speed is a public–private partnership initiated by the U.S. government to facilitate and accelerate the development, manufacturing, and distribution of COVID-19 vaccines, therapeutics, and diagnostics. The program was funded in March 2020 with $10 billion from the CARES[46] Act passed by U.S. Congress.

Blockchain is a distributed ledger technology (DLT) that allows data to be stored globally on thousands of servers – while letting anyone on the network see everyone else's entries in near real-time. This methodology is defined in detail in **Chapter 4.**

[46] Coronavirus Aid, Relief, and Economic Security

Blockchains on page 123.

The use of blockchain technology for Operation Warp Speed ensures optimum utilization of resources to save precious lives, without compromising quality or safety. DLT has seen pockets of implementation in federal health agencies in prior years, but it was not fully embraced until the complexities of securely tracing the distribution of COVID-19 vaccine from manufacturing by Pfizer or Moderna all the way to delivery to patients.

Management of this supply chain faces monumental challenges across the world since it will be distributed to hundreds of millions of people by multiple parties over a long period of time. Consumers want transparency about the source of their products and their security thoughout the supply chain life cycle.

Major providers of blockchain technology services for logistics are:

- **Accenture PLC** operates its business through segments such as Financial Services, Products, and Others. The company offers blockchain technology solutions for the transportation and logistics industry.
- **Capgemini Services SAS** operates its business through segments such as Strategy & Transformation, Applications & Technology, and Operations & Engineering. The company offers blockchain technology solutions for the transportation and logistics industry.
- **Infosys Ltd** operates its business through segments such as Energy, Utilities, Resources and Services, Manufacturing, Hi-Tech, Life Sciences, and All other segments. The company offers blockchain technology solutions for the transportation and logistics industry.
- **IBM** unveiled "Blockchain as a Service" in March 2017. The technology is based upon open source Hyperledger Fabric developed in public domain[47] by The Linux Foundation.

---

[47] software placed in public domain has absolutely no ownership such as copyright, trademark, or patent.

There are two software development foundations for developing software to support blockchain technology. Hyperledger leverages blockchain technology for business, while Ethereum runs software for decentralized mass consumption.

Supply chain tracking, tracing, and responsiveness is significantly improved when employing blockchain technology for logistics. Blockchains in the supply chain have four essential characteristics: **decentralized consensus, information sharing, incentivizing** and **negotiation**. This technology provides substantial capabilities that no other system can provide: transparency, traceability, security, real-time data, and smart contracts. Other technologies, such as physical internet, RFID[48], cloud computing, sensors, and others, can be combined with the technology.

Within a blockchain environment, data is stored in blocks that are chained in a shared immutable ledger as they continue to grow. Each block has a timestamp and a link to its previous block that cannot be modified once it has been recorded. At all times, the data is transparently accessible to the supply chain participants. Such a collaborated effort for information sharing improves traceability in both global and local supply chain scenarios.

There are three paramount requirements for managing the logistics for ultimate delivery of the vaccine to patients. They are Localization, Agility and Digitation of the supply chain. This enables a "circular economy", as shown below.

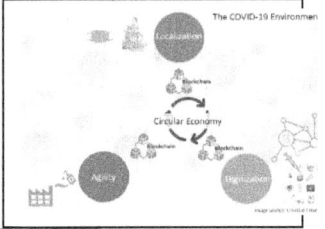

---

[48] Radio-frequency identification

Localization

The COVID crisis unveiled the fragility of global supply chains. Localized sourcing became important due to high demand and the need for expedited delivery. This was caused in part by the United States restricting the export of products and materials from China *(and vice-versa)*. There was a concern about spreading the virus through packaging. Localization of supplies maintains competitiveness and reduces freight costs and risk of loss. Local area businesses can respond quickly and generally have sufficient inventory on hand with good replenishment practices.

Agility

Agility is the ability to meet customer demand combined with the ability to compete within rapid market changes. Blockchains bring **trust** into the equation. Agility improves sensitivity to everchanging markets, access to shared information and integration of capabilities to resolve demand needs. Agility requires rapid response to unpredictable changes to supply or demand. In manufacturing, agility can be viewed as the ability to perceive changes as opportunities. It enables rapid implementation of operational changes and entrepreneurial alterness.

Digitization

Digitization enables programmable logic for providing commodities and services while socially isolated. It facilitates online purchases and delivery of goods. It removes physical boundaries of time, distance and function. It is a powerful platform for building brand recognition (i.e., Prime) and strengthening relationship by digitially connecting large numbers of people while recording their "likes" and the demographics within which they move.

The Supply Chain

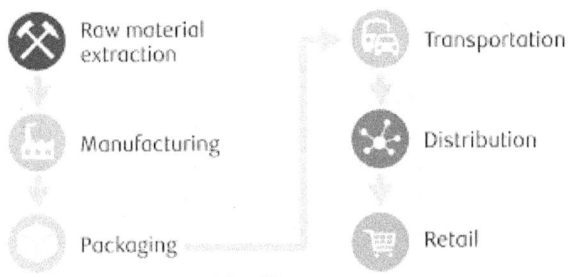

Challenges

In December 2020, two vaccines were approved for emergency use and mass distribution. They are the Pfizer/BioNTech vaccine and Moderna's vaccine.

There are monumental challenges to be met:

> - Each of the vaccines that have been approved or are soon to be approved for emergency use requires two doses. In order to achieve herd immunity throughout the world, 15 billion does would have to be manufactured, distributed, delivered and monitored throughout the supply chain.
> - The two front-runners require refrigeration until they have been administered. Pfizer's vaccine needs to be refrigerated at minus 70 degrees Celsius *(which is colder than winter in Antarctica)*. Moderna's vaccine needs to be kept at minus 20 degrees Celsius *(more like a regular freezer)*.
> - Pfizer's vaccine, which it developed with <u>BioNTech SE</u>, must be kept at ultracold temperatures in specialized freezers and containers, and stored at 70 degrees below zero Celsius (-94 degrees Fahrenheit).
> - A very small percentage of inoculated patients suffer severe allergy symptoms. The CDC has recommended that people who have had a severe allergic reaction to any ingriedient in a COVID-19 vaccine should not get that manufacturer's vaccine.
> -

➢ The Bottom Line

The implementation of blockchain in the COVID-19 vaccine supply chain will ensure the transparency of standards followed at each step by creating an exact copy of the ledger at every node in the network. Blockchain being a decentralized technology, the ledger in the network is public and maintained by all users, giving a transparent view at each level. Anything that needs to be added to the ledger is required to be validated by every node.

Blockchain not only improves the supply chain and logistics process but also ensures authentication of the healthcare workers' identity, maintenance of patient records, and tracking of the treatment aftereffects.

Blockchain also acts as a supervisor for healthcare centers to check instances of staffers exploiting their authority or compromising on their responsibility.

Blockchain technology is the best, and possibly only, platform for efficiently monitoring and managing the COVID-19 vaccine supply chain. Blockchain offers an immutable, decentralized database that can assure that vaccine supplies are being stored and handled properly, while tracking every transaction in the process.

Blockchain technology allows multiple parties to manage and share a decentralized database. These parties can create and share a transparent source of truth that can be mutually agreed upon.

As a result, blockchain is the perfect infrastructure for supply chain management because it addresses two key pre-requisites requirements for building digital trust:

- ➢ It is not owned by anyone, but rather provides a generic standardized protocol within which all participants along the chain can connect and share relevant data.
- ➢ It is immutable. Therefore, existing information cannot be deleted, but only appended. This drives a higher level of accountability by each participant who writes new data.

Epilogue

I am confident that by 2035, the active and working generation will look back at 2018 *(when this book was first published)* and wonder why we had bank accounts and checkbooks and why it was necessary to sign a paper contract when we rented a car or lodging, or bought a home. They will no longer see CPAs as auditors or use humans as tax preparers, bookkeepers or drivers. They probably will not even carry currency in their wallets *(if they still carry a wallet or a purse)*. If in 2018 you are still under 35, be prepared to be disrupted by blockchain technology over your next thirty years.

With persistent blockchain technology in place for most commercial activities, we will have transcended from distributing wealth to distributing value and opportunity across our society. Immutable records will have eliminated fraud and identity theft. Widespread remittance scams imposed by middlemen will have been eliminated. Society in 2035 will witness accountable governments and regulators who oversee transparent smart contracts within a truly democratic model worldwide.

A

Acorn · 36
Ada Lovelace · 27
Affectiva · 78
AidCoin · 128
Alan Turing · 38
ALGOL · 40
Altair · 36
Apple · 36, 49
Archimedes · 15
Archytas · 44
Aristotle · 44
Arithometer · 8
Atlant · 120
ATS · 116
ATS token · 116
Authorship · 116

B

BaaS · 105, 106, 107, 118, 126, 128, 129
Babylonian · 9
Backus · 30
Bank of America · 130
Beyond Verbal · 78
Bitcoin Cash · 90
blockchain · 80, 83, 89, 91, 101, 102, 103, 104, 105, 108, 113, 121, 122, 126, 130, 132, 142
BSP · 107

C

Charles Babbage · 11, 14, 16, 27
COBOL · 28
Coinbase · 96

Corda · 119

D

DARPA · 61, 76
Douglas Engelbart · 33
DRAM · 33
Durov, Pavel and Nikolai · 107

E

Elixir · 134
Elmer Sperry · 54
ENIAC · 22, 24
Ethereum · 89, 90, 91, 94, 110, 116, 117, 131, 134, 135
Etherium · 89

F

FORTRAN · 30

G

Gartner · 126
Gary Powers · 55
George Boole · 12
George Stibitz · 23
Goodmall · 120
Grace Hopper · 28
gram · 107

H

Haber, Stuart · **98**
Hal Finney · 80

Her · 27, 72
HitBTC · 116
Hollerith · 16, 17
Hyperledger · 105, 106
Hyperledger Project · 105

I

IBM · 17, 25, 26, 30, 31, 33, 36, 37, 41, 42, 61, 66, 76, 77, 104, 105, 106, 121, 125, 147
Intel · 33, 34, 36
Isaac Asimov · 44
Ishanga · 15
Ivy Koin · 96

J

J.V. Atanasoff · 21
Jack Kilby · 33
Jacquard · 8, 14, 16
Jacquard, Frances · 8
Java · 31
Joaquin Phoenix · 72
John Mauchly · 22, 24
John McCarthy · 40

K

Kaleido · 118
Karel Capek · 44
Kennedy · 55
Kickstarter · 60, 133, 134
Kinect · 78
Komodo · 133
Kurzweil · 14, 62, 65, 66, 67

L

Leonardo Da Vinci · 44
LISP · 40
Litecoin · 89

M

Maersk · 121
Mayan · 9
Modha · 77
Moore's law · 34
Mycelia · 116, 117

N

Nakamoto · 80, 81, 98
NEAC · 25
Nikola Tesla · 44
Noam Chomsky · 40

O

OMG · 131
OmiseGo · 130

P

Pem · 19, 20
Phantom · 56
Phil Savenick · 18, 19
Philo Farnsworth · 18
Pierre Jaquet-Droz · 44
PL/1 · 31
Presper Eckert · 22, 24
punch cards · 14, 16, 17, 28

Pythagoras · 15

Q

Quipu · 8

R

R3 · 118
Relativity Space · 60
Ripple · 89, 130
Robert Noyce · 33, 34

S

SABRE · 26
Samuel Williams · 23
Sawtooth · 118
Scarlett Johansson · 72
Sculpteo · 59
Selfkey · 115
Silicon Valley Bank · 95
singularity · 14, 65, 66
smart contracts · 89, 91, 116, 118, 135
Smart Contracts · 108
Stanley Kubrick · 69
Stephen Hawking · 53
Steve Jobs · 36
Steve Wozniak · 36
Stornetta, W. Scott · 98
Stratasys · 60
Szabo, Nick · 108

T

Telegram · 107
Thomas de Colmar, Charles · 8
Tom Frey · 57
TradeIX · 119
transistors · 32
triode · 32
True North · 66
TrueEX · 92
True-North · 76
Turing · 7, 23, 30, 38, 41, 64, 66, 78
Turing, Alan · 7

U

Ujo Music · 116, 117
Ultrum · 133
UNIVAC · 24
Upbit · 85

V

von Neumann · 14, 77

W

Watson · 41, 42
William Shockley · 33

ABOUT THE AUTHOR

After graduating from the U.S. Coast Guard Academy with a degree in Marine Engineering, Pete served as an officer on several assignments in the Pacific and in California. During his six years in the Coast Guard, he was Commanding Officer of two Coast Guard units.

His information technology career includes systems design and development positions at IBM, EDS and Chevron. Pete served in project management roles designing, developing, and managing major financial systems projects at Chevron and Household Financial Services.

Presently, Pete provides business consulting services to businesses, large and small, in many industries. His focus is in integrating his clients' business applications seamlessly with their web sites and other installed business applications. Many of Pete's clients are wineries. He also serves manufacturers and distributors with complex inventory management and logistics requirements.

Pete continues to be consumed by advances in artificial intelligence, machine learning, voice recognition and neural technology.

www.ingramcontent.com/pod-product-compliance
Lightning Source LLC
Chambersburg PA
CBHW070642220526
45466CB00001B/258